A COOKBOOK PUBLISHED BY DAIRY DIARY

Retro Classics

A JOYFUL COLLECTION OF NOSTALGIC RECIPES,
UPDATED FOR TODAY'S COOK

DAIRY DIARY
COOK
BOOK

Contents

INTRODUCTION	4
RECIPE NOTES	6
APPETISERS & SNACKS	**8**
Cheese Straws	11
Creamed Mushrooms	12
French Onion Soup with Cheese Toasts	15
Leek & Potato Soup (Also Vichyssoise)	16
Split Pea & Ham Soup	19
Coronation Chicken Sandwiches	20
Welsh Rarebit (Also Buck Rarebit)	23
Potted Shrimps (Also Potted Beef)	24
MAIN MEALS	**26**
Cauliflower Cheese (Also Macaroni Cheese)	29
Bubble & Squeak	30
Pan Haggerty	33
Potato & Cheese Pie	34
Vegetarian Moussaka	37
Veggie Burgers	38
Cod with Parsley Sauce (Also Cod with Butter Sauce)	41
Finnan Haddock	42
Family Fish Pie	45
Scampi & Chips	46
Chicken Curry (Also Vegetable Curry)	49
Chicken Kiev	50
Coq au Vin	53
Leek & Bacon Stovies	54
Quiche Lorraine (Also Broccoli & Stilton Quiche, Leek & Cheese Quiche)	57
Crispy Pancakes	58
Ham with Pease Pudding	61
Toad-in-the-Hole	62
Sausage & Leek Supper	65
Sausage & Pickle Pie	66
Liver & Bacon with Onion Gravy	69
Roast Lamb with Fresh Mint Sauce	70
Lancashire Hotpot	73
Shepherd's Pie	74
Corned Beef Hash	77
Farmhouse Mince	78
Mince & Onion Pie	81
Teviotdale Pie	82
Lobby	85
Beef Stroganoff	86
Steak & Kidney Pudding	89
Steak Diane	90
PUDDINGS	**92**
Tutti Frutti Ice Cream	95
Arctic Roll (Also Chocolate Ice Cream Roll)	96
Blancmange	99

Butterscotch Delight	100
Fruit Pavlova	103
Summer Pudding (Also Autumn Pudding)	104
Strawberry Trifle (Also Pear & Ginger Trifle, Black Forest Trifle, Raspberry & Amaretti Trifle)	107
Chocolate Bar Cheesecake	108
Black Forest Gateau	111
Lemon Meringue Pie	112
Coconut Jam Sponge Pudding	115
Eve's Pudding	116
Pineapple Upside Down Pudding (Also Chocolate Upside Down Pudding)	119
Syrup Sponge Pudding (Also Chocolate Sponge Pudding, Fruit Sponge Pudding, Jam Sponge Pudding)	120
Jam Roly Poly (Also Syrup Roly Poly, Lemon Roly Poly, Mincemeat Roly Poly, Spotted Dick or Dog)	123
Chocolate Pudding	124
School Chocolate Cracknel with Pink, Green or Chocolate Custard	127
Rice Pudding (Also Tapioca Pudding, Semolina Pudding, Sago Pudding)	128
Baked Custards	131
Bread & Butter Pudding (Also Osborne Pudding)	132
Fruit Crumble	135

Butterscotch Apple Pie	136
Treacle Tart	139
BAKES & TREATS	**140**
Bakewell Tart	142
Manchester Tart	145
Fruit Slice (Fly Pie)	146
Choc Mint Bars	149
Cherry Coconut Choc Traybake	150
Shrewsbury Biscuits	153
Rock Cakes	154
Tottenham Cake	157
Pineapple & Coconut Fruit Loaf	158
Hedgehog Celebration Cake (Also Sweetshop Celebration Cake)	161
Boiled Fruit Christmas Cake	162
Krispie Cakes	165
Tiffin	166
Peppermint Creams (Also Chocolate Peppermint Creams)	169
White Chocolate Fudge (Also Chocolate Bar Fudge, Milk Chocolate Fudge)	169
Coconut Ice	170
Butterscotch	170
INDEX	**172**
ACKNOWLEDGEMENTS	**176**

Introduction

Flavour is incredibly emotive, and a taste of something
familiar can take you right back to a time and place.

You may remember being allowed to lick
the spoon in the kitchen as a child, eating
pudding in the school hall, a particular meal
at your own dining table, or other tastes
that reconnect you with the past. Many
flavours evoke happy memories and you'll
discover plenty in this wonderful collection
of timeless classics, requested by thousands
of our readers.

What and how we cook has changed
dramatically over the centuries, but some
dishes have stood the test of time. Trifle,
for example, was first published in the 16th
century, Toad-in-the-Hole in the 1700s
and Jam Roly Poly in Victorian times,
printed in Mrs Beeton's *Book of Household
Management*. The original *Dairy Book of
Home Cookery*, published in the sixties,
included many recipes we now consider
retro, with pies, tarts, milk puddings, and
even a cheese & pineapple porcupine – the
party essential!

The recipes in *Retro Classics* have been
chosen following the results from a survey
of 40,000 people, which asked for their
most fondly remembered dishes. Each has
been tested three times (some many more!)
and updated to ensure that it uses readily
available ingredients, simple cooking methods
to save you time and, most importantly, tastes
delicious. Some will be fabulously familiar,
while others may be new to you and become
favourites of the future.

Every recipe has been beautifully
photographed, with a variety of vintage
cloths, crockery and cookware, some of
which you may remember (or still have!).
The result is a joyful compendium of nostalgic
classics, which will raise a smile as you flick
through the pages. Many of the dishes will
become a talking point with friends and
family as they too recollect their favourites.
Retro Classics is a genuinely delightful book
and will inspire you to cook, chat and share.

Recipe Notes

For each recipe, there's an introduction, describing the origins of the dish, followed by the number of servings and time it takes to prepare and cook. And some show the following symbols:

V Suitable for vegetarians
(if using suitable cheeses, yogurts etc.)
F Suitable for freezing

In Dairy Diary cookbook style, the ingredients are shown first, so that you can easily glance through the list to see what is needed. The method is simple and logical to follow.

Spoon measures are level unless otherwise stated.

Large eggs are used in testing, but it's usually fine to use whatever size eggs you have to hand.

Useful tips are given, and some recipes have variations so that you can tweak the recipe and create different dishes.

Where the recipe can be cooked in an air fryer (without changing tin sizes or batch-cooking), we have given instructions.

Nutritional information follows government guidelines and is calculated by portion/item. Where there are variations, e.g. serves 6–8, the analysis is based on the larger number. Sugar refers to how much of the carbohydrate comes from sugars. These are 'total sugars', which include 'free' (added) sugars and sugars naturally present in whole fruit, vegetables and milk.

Safety

Recipes using nut products are not suitable for young children or those with a nut allergy. Certain at-risk groups, such as pregnant women, babies and sick or elderly people, should not eat raw or lightly cooked eggs. Ovens vary, so always check that food, especially meat, is thoroughly cooked before serving.

Appetisers & Snacks

11   CHEESE STRAWS

12   CREAMED MUSHROOMS

15   FRENCH ONION SOUP WITH CHEESE TOASTS

16   LEEK & POTATO SOUP
     (ALSO VICHYSSOISE)

19   SPLIT PEA & HAM SOUP

20   CORONATION CHICKEN SANDWICHES

23   WELSH RAREBIT
     (ALSO BUCK RAREBIT)

24   POTTED SHRIMPS
     (ALSO POTTED BEEF)

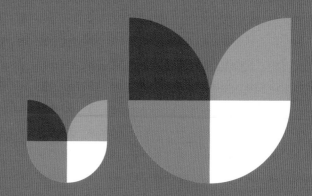

Cheese Straws

A savoury course, such as cheese straws, was often served after dessert in well-to-do households in the late nineteenth and early twentieth centuries. By the 1960s cheese straws had come back into fashion as a party snack popular with children and adults alike.

MAKES 20   **PREPARATION** 15 minutes   **COOKING** 15–18 minutes

Butter for greasing
Mature Cheddar cheese 75g (3oz), grated
Paprika ½ tsp

Cayenne pepper ½ tsp (optional)
Salt and freshly ground black pepper
Ready-rolled puff pastry 320g pack
Egg 1 medium, beaten

1 Preheat the oven to 200°C/180°fan/ Gas 6. Grease a baking sheet.
2 Mix together the cheese, paprika, cayenne pepper, if using, and seasoning.
3 Lay the pastry on a sheet of baking paper and brush with egg. Sprinkle with the cheese mixture and gently press onto the pastry.
4 Cut in half lengthways, then cut each half into 2–3cm (¾–1in) strips. Gently twist each strip and place on the prepared baking sheet. Brush with egg, then bake for 15–18 minutes until crisp and golden.
5 Cool on a wire rack, then store in an airtight container for up to a week.

TIPS
Use a mixture of Italian-style hard cheese and Cheddar if you prefer. If cooking for vegetarians, make sure the cheeses are suitable.
You could add finely chopped nuts such as pecans or walnuts.

Calories	Fibre	Salt	Sugar	Fat
83	0.5g	0.2g	0.2g	6g of which 3g is saturated

Creamed Mushrooms

Puff pastry cases, or vol au vents, were created by the French chef Carême in the early 1800s. His vol au vents – so light they 'flew away in the wind' – became famous throughout Europe and have stood the test of time; they are usually filled with a creamy mixture, such as creamed mushrooms.

SERVES 6   **PREPARATION** 10 minutes   **COOKING** 15 minutes

Butter 50g (2oz)
Button mushrooms 700g (1½lb), wiped and halved
Onion 1, peeled and finely chopped
Plain flour 2 tbsp
Milk 300ml (½ pint)
Egg yolks 2

Dry sherry 3 tbsp or **soy sauce** 2 tbsp
Cayenne pepper ¼ tsp
Ground nutmeg pinch
Salt and freshly ground black pepper
Ready-made vol au vents 18 or **freshly made toast**

1 In a large frying pan, heat half the butter and fry the mushrooms and onion until tender. Drain well.
2 Put the remaining butter, flour and milk in a saucepan and bring to the boil, whisking constantly, then simmer for 2 minutes until thickened.
3 Over a low heat, whisk in the egg yolks, sherry or soy sauce, cayenne pepper, nutmeg, salt and pepper, then add the mushrooms and onion and stir for 2 minutes until hot.
4 Spoon into vol au vent cases or onto toast and serve immediately.

TIPS
When served in vol au vent cases this is perfect for a buffet, or spoon onto some freshly toasted sourdough for a delicious lunch. You could sprinkle with chopped parsley or snipped salad cress to finish.

Calories	Fibre	Salt	Sugar	Fat
382	3g	1.3g	5g	25g of which 13g is saturated

French Onion Soup with Cheese Toasts

This classic French soup became famous as a restorative served to workers at Les Halles food market in nineteenth-century Paris. The market opened very early in the morning, so it was often the last port of call for party-goers, who found the onion soup was a great way to ward off hangovers. In the 1960s it became a staple of bistros in the UK and USA.

SERVES 4   **PREPARATION** 10 minutes   **COOKING** 55 minutes   F

Butter 25g (1oz)
Onions 350g (12oz), peeled and thinly sliced
Beef stock 900ml (1½ pints)

Salt and freshly ground black pepper
Dry sherry 2 tsp (optional)
Baguette 4 slices, each 2.5cm (1in) thick
Cheddar cheese 25g (1oz), grated

1 Melt the butter in a large saucepan and gently fry the onions for about 5 minutes or until golden.
2 Pour in the beef stock and season to taste. Bring to the boil, then lower the heat, cover and simmer for 45 minutes.
3 Add the sherry, if using. Preheat the grill to medium.
4 Lightly toast the baguette slices on both sides, then sprinkle with cheese and grill until bubbling.
5 Ladle the soup into warmed bowls and top each with a cheese toast.

TIPS
Spread the toast with a little mustard before sprinkling with the cheese, if you like. Top with Gruyère cheese rather than Cheddar. If you have fresh thyme, add a couple of sprigs while the soup is cooking. Alternatively, sprinkle with torn fresh oregano to finish.

AIR FRYER
Step 4, place the baguette slices in the air fryer drawer, sprinkle with cheese and air fry at 180°C for 5 minutes or until bubbling.

Calories	Fibre	Salt	Sugar	Fat
186	3g	2g	6g	8g of which 5g is saturated

Leek & Potato Soup

A simple soup that will never go out of fashion,
with its classic garnish of cream and chives.

SERVES 4-6   **PREPARATION** 10 minutes   **COOKING** 30-40 minutes

Butter 25g (1oz)
Leeks 2, trimmed and sliced
Onion 1 small, peeled and chopped
Potatoes 350g (12oz), peeled and
thinly sliced

1 Melt the butter in a large saucepan and
gently fry the leeks and onion for 7-10
minutes without browning.
2 Add the potatoes, chicken stock, salt,
pepper and nutmeg or mace. Bring to
the boil, then cover and simmer for
20-30 minutes until the vegetables are
tender.
3 Whizz the soup with a stick blender.
Ladle into warmed bowls and add a swirl
of cream and a sprinkle of chives, if using.

Chicken stock 600ml (1 pint)
Salt and freshly ground black pepper
Ground nutmeg or mace ¼ tsp
Double cream 4-6 tbsp
Snipped chives to garnish (optional)

TIP
If you don't have a stick blender, pour
into a liquidiser to purée the soup.

VARIATION
■ **Vichyssoise** Cool and chill for 3-4
hours. Serve cold.

Calories	Fibre	Salt	Sugar	Fat
232	3g	1.3g	3g	17g of which 11g is saturated

Split Pea & Ham Soup

Tasty and filling, this soup is sometimes called London Particular, referring to the thick fogs or 'pea soupers' that regularly blanketed London during the nineteenth century and well into the twentieth.

SERVES 2   **PREPARATION** 15 minutes   **COOKING** 2¼ hours

Split peas 110g (4oz), rinsed and drained
Pork or ham stock 900ml (1½ pints)
Butter 25g (1oz)
Onion 1, peeled and chopped
Celery 1 stick, chopped

Potato 1, peeled and finely chopped
Lean ham 50g (2oz), chopped
Freshly ground black pepper
Finely chopped parsley 1–2 tbsp
(optional)

1 Put the split peas in a large saucepan and pour in the stock. Bring to the boil, then cover and simmer gently for 1 hour, stirring occasionally.
2 Melt the butter in a frying pan and fry the onion, celery and potato for about 5 minutes or until softened.
3 Add the onion mixture to the peas with the ham and simmer for a further hour, stirring occasionally.
4 Season to taste with pepper. Leave the soup chunky or purée with a stick blender if you prefer. Ladle into warmed bowls and serve with a sprinkle of parsley, if using.

TIPS
Instead of onion, celery and potato, you could use a ready-prepared frozen soffritto mix. You can soak the split peas for at least 1 hour, or overnight, and reduce the cooking time if you like.
For a one-pan soup, omit the butter and onion, and add the chopped celery and potato to the pan after the first hour.

Calories	Fibre	Salt	Sugar	Fat
442	9g	4.8g	7g	14g of which 8g is saturated

Coronation Chicken Sandwiches

Coronation chicken was created for a lunch celebrating the coronation of Queen Elizabeth II in 1953. At the time, with rationing still in place, it would have seemed quite exotic. It's evolved over the years and is now best known as a sandwich filling – perfect for using leftover cooked chicken.

SERVES 2 **PREPARATION** 15 minutes

Greek-style yogurt 2 tbsp
Mayonnaise 3 tbsp
Mango chutney 1 tsp
Curry powder ¼–½ tsp
Salt and freshly ground black pepper
Cooked chicken 175g (6oz), shredded
Celery 1 stick, finely chopped

Sultanas 1 heaped tbsp
Toasted flaked almonds 1 heaped tbsp (optional)
Crusty farmhouse white loaf 4 slices
Butter for spreading
Salad cress, snipped

1 Mix together the yogurt, mayonnaise, mango chutney, curry powder, salt and pepper.
2 Stir through the shredded chicken, celery, sultanas and flaked almonds, if using.
3 Butter each slice of bread and divide the filling between two slices.
4 Sprinkle over the snipped cress and top with the remaining slices of bread. Cut each sandwich in half and serve immediately.

TIPS
Start with the smaller amount of curry powder, taste and add more if you prefer. For a vegetarian version, use Quorn instead of chicken.

Calories	Fibre	Salt	Sugar	Fat
645	2.5g	1.3g	17g	35g of which 10g is saturated

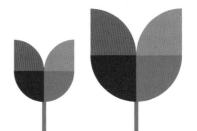

Welsh Rarebit

Originally known as Welsh rabbit, perhaps dating to times when cheese was used as a replacement for meat. The term 'rarebit' was first recorded in 1785 and ever since there has been much discussion over which is the 'correct' name.

SERVES 4   **PREPARATION** 7 minutes   **COOKING** 7 minutes

Butter 25g (1oz)
Plain flour 2 tbsp
English mustard ½ tsp
Worcestershire sauce ½ tsp
Ale 125ml (4fl oz)

Caerphilly, Lancashire or Cheddar cheese 110g (4oz), grated
Milk 2 tbsp
Bread 4 large slices
Tomatoes and salad cress to serve (optional)

1 Preheat the grill to medium-hot.
2 Melt the butter in a saucepan and whisk in the flour, mustard and Worcestershire sauce.
3 Gradually whisk in the ale and cook, stirring, until you have a thick sauce.
4 Add the cheese and milk stir until the cheese has melted.
5 Toast the slices of bread on one side only. Spread the untoasted side with the cheese mixture, then grill until browned and bubbling. Serve with tomatoes and salad cress, if liked.

TIP
You could replace the English mustard with wholegrain, if preferred.

VARIATION
■ **Buck Rarebit** Serve each slice with a poached egg on top.

Calories	Fibre	Salt	Sugar	Fat
284	1g	1g	2.5g	15g of which 9g is saturated

Potted Shrimps, Potted Beef

Before the advent of refrigeration, potting was a way to preserve a wide range of food such as fish and shellfish, meat and game. Potted shrimps or potted beef – a delicious way to use leftover roast beef – make a superb first course or light lunch or supper.

SERVES 4   **PREPARATION** 20 minutes plus setting and chilling   **COOKING** 5 minutes

■ **Potted Shrimps**
Clarified butter (below)
Shrimps 250–300g (9–11oz), shelled weight
Ground nutmeg pinch
Ground mace pinch
Salt and freshly ground black pepper

1 Melt half of the clarified butter and stir in the remaining ingredients. Divide the mixture between four small ramekin dishes or small glass jars. Chill until the mixture has set.
2 Melt the remaining clarified butter and spoon over the top of the dishes. Chill until the butter has set.
3 Serve with melba toast or freshly toasted bread.

■ **Potted Beef**
Clarified butter (below)
Cooked roast beef 250g (9oz), finely shredded or whizzed in a food processor
Horseradish sauce 1 tsp
Salt and freshly ground black pepper

■ **Clarified Butter** Melt 110g (4oz) butter in a small saucepan over a very low heat and then leave it in the fridge to set for 10–15 minutes. Carefully pour the clear butter into a jug or bowl and discard the milky liquid underneath.

■ **Melba Toast** Preheat the grill and toast sliced bread on both sides. Using a serrated knife, cut off the crusts, then slide the knife through the centre of the toast to split it into two thin pieces. Cut each piece into four triangles and place under the grill again, untoasted side uppermost, until golden and the edges curl.

Calories	Fibre	Salt	Sugar	Fat	Potted Shrimps
253	0.3g	2g	0.2g	23g of which 14g is saturated	

Calories	Fibre	Salt	Sugar	Fat	Potted Beef
318	0.1g	1.1g	0.5g	26g of which 16g is saturated	

Main Meals

29 CAULIFLOWER CHEESE
    (ALSO MACARONI CHEESE)

30 BUBBLE & SQUEAK

33 PAN HAGGERTY

34 POTATO & CHEESE PIE

37 VEGETARIAN MOUSSAKA

38 VEGGIE BURGERS

41 COD WITH PARSLEY SAUCE
    (ALSO COD WITH BUTTER SAUCE)

42 FINNAN HADDOCK

45 FAMILY FISH PIE

46 SCAMPI & CHIPS

49 CHICKEN CURRY
    (ALSO VEGETABLE CURRY)

50 CHICKEN KIEV

53 COQ AU VIN

54 LEEK & BACON STOVIES

57 QUICHE LORRAINE
    (ALSO BROCCOLI & STILTON QUICHE,
    LEEK & CHEESE QUICHE)

58 CRISPY PANCAKES

61 HAM WITH PEASE PUDDING

62 TOAD-IN-THE-HOLE

65 SAUSAGE & LEEK SUPPER

66 SAUSAGE & PICKLE PIE

69 LIVER & BACON WITH ONION GRAVY

70 ROAST LAMB WITH FRESH MINT SAUCE

73 LANCASHIRE HOTPOT

74 SHEPHERD'S PIE

77 CORNED BEEF HASH

78 FARMHOUSE MINCE

81 MINCE & ONION PIE

82 TEVIOTDALE PIE

85 LOBBY

86 BEEF STROGANOFF

89 STEAK & KIDNEY PUDDING

90 STEAK DIANE

Cauliflower Cheese

A comforting family favourite, topped with
panko breadcrumbs for an extra crispy finish.

SERVES 2 as a main meal or 4 as a side   **PREPARATION** 10 minutes
COOKING 20–25 minutes   Ⓥ

Cauliflower 1, cut into florets
Butter 25g (1oz)
Plain flour 25g (1oz)
Milk 300ml (½ pint)
Salt and freshly ground black pepper
Dijon mustard ½ tsp

Cheddar cheese 110g (4oz), grated
Panko breadcrumbs 25g (1oz)
New potatoes and peas to serve
(optional)

1 Preheat the oven to 200°C/180°fan/
Gas 6.
2 Cook the cauliflower in a pan of salted
boiling water for 4–5 minutes until just
tender. Drain well and transfer to a
baking dish.
3 Meanwhile, put the butter, flour and
milk in a saucepan and bring to the boil,
whisking continuously, then simmer,
whisking, for 2–3 minutes until smooth
and thick. Remove from the heat, season
to taste and whisk in the mustard and
half of the grated cheese. Pour the
cheese sauce over the cauliflower.
4 Mix the remaining cheese with the
breadcrumbs, then sprinkle over the
cauliflower.
5 Bake for 10–15 minutes until the cheese
and breadcrumbs are golden.
6 Serve immediately as a side dish
or with new potatoes and peas for
a main meal.

VARIATION
■ **Macaroni Cheese** Replace the
cauliflower with 350g (12oz) dried
macaroni and cook according to the
packet instructions.

Calories	Fibre	Salt	Sugar	Fat	Based on 2 servings
591	6g	2.2g	16g	37g of which 22g is saturated	

Bubble & Squeak

It's often said that the name comes from the sounds of cooking: the vegetables first bubbling as they boil and then squeaking in the frying pan. Serve with a chilli sauce, ketchup or chutney, or with a poached or fried egg, for breakfast, brunch, lunch or supper.

SERVES 2   **PREPARATION** 5 minutes   **COOKING** 20 minutes

Butter 25g (1oz)
Onion 1, peeled and finely chopped
Cooked mashed potatoes 450g (1lb)
Cooked cabbage 225g (8oz), finely chopped

Cooked roast beef 4–8 slices, chopped
Salt and freshly ground black pepper

1 Melt the butter in a large frying pan. Add the onion and cook for 4–5 minutes, stirring frequently, until softened.
2 Add the potatoes, cabbage and beef. Season to taste. Fry over medium heat for about 15 minutes, stirring frequently, until browned. Serve hot.

TIPS

Bubble and squeak traditionally uses leftovers from the previous day's roast dinner. Replace the beef with leftover lamb if you prefer. Feel free to add other leftover cooked vegetables, such as parsnips, carrots, Brussels sprouts or kale.

Calories	Fibre	Salt	Sugar	Fat
516	9g	1.5g	11g	21g of which 10g is saturated

Pan Haggerty

This traditional Northumbrian dish of layers of potatoes, onion and cheese, browned under the grill, makes a filling one-pan supper.

SERVES 2 as a main meal or 4 as a side   **PREPARATION** 15 minutes
COOKING 25–35 minutes Ⓥ

Butter 25g (1oz)
Sunflower oil 1 tbsp
Potatoes 500g (1lb 2oz), peeled and thinly sliced

Onion 1, peeled and sliced
Salt and freshly ground black pepper
Lancashire cheese 110g (4oz), grated

1 Heat the butter and oil in a heavy-based frying pan until the butter has melted.
2 Remove the pan from the heat and add a layer of potatoes, then a layer of onion, seasoning each layer well. Add a layer of cheese, then repeat the layers, finishing with cheese.
3 Cover the pan with a lid or foil and cook over a low heat for 20–30 minutes or until the potatoes and onion are tender when pierced with the point of a thin knife.
4 Preheat the grill to hot.
5 Remove the cover and put the pan under the hot grill to brown the top. Serve straight from the pan.

TIP
For non-vegetarians, add some chopped ham or cooked bacon to the layers.

AIR FRYER
Brush the air fryer drawer with melted butter and oil then layer the potatoes, onions and cheese into the drawer and air fry at 180°C for 30 minutes or until tender.

Calories	Fibre	Salt	Sugar	Fat
583	7g	1.8g	7g	34g of which 18g is saturated

Potato & Cheese Pie

No pastry, no fuss, a budget-friendly meat-free bake that was promoted during the Second World War – perhaps with less cheese! – and has remained a popular family supper ever since.

SERVES 4   **PREPARATION** 15 minutes   **COOKING** 35 minutes

Potatoes 750g (1lb 8oz), peeled and cut into chunks
Butter 25g (1oz), plus extra for greasing
Onion 1, peeled and finely chopped
Milk 4 tbsp
Egg 1, beaten
Mustard 1 tsp

Yeast extract ½ tsp
Finely chopped parsley 3 tbsp
Double Gloucester cheese 175g (6oz), grated
Salt and freshly ground black pepper
Steamed vegetables or baked beans to serve

1 Put the potatoes in a pan of cold water and bring to the boil, then simmer for 15–20 minutes until just tender. Drain well.

2 Meanwhile, melt the butter in a pan. Add the onion and cook for 4–5 minutes, stirring frequently, until softened.

3 Preheat the oven to 220°C/200°fan/Gas 7. Butter a 1.2 litre (2 pint) baking dish.

4 Mash the potatoes with the milk, egg, mustard and yeast extract, then stir in the onion, parsley and 110g (4oz) of the cheese. Season to taste with salt and pepper.

5 Transfer the mixture to the prepared baking dish. Sprinkle the remaining cheese over the top. Bake for 15 minutes or until golden brown.

6 Serve hot with freshly cooked vegetables or baked beans.

TIPS

If you prefer, you can soften the onion with a splash of water in the microwave for 1 minute.

Marmite is the most commonly known yeast extract.

AIR FRYER

Step 5, put the potato mixture straight into the air fryer drawer and air fry at 180°C for 10 minutes or until golden.

Calories	Fibre	Salt	Sugar	Fat
438	5g	1.6g	5g	24g of which 14g is saturated

Vegetarian Moussaka

Aubergines originate in South Asia, but for over 1000 years have been grown in countries around the Mediterranean. When more people began to enjoy foreign holidays in the 1960s, moussaka became a popular dish on British dinner tables and it has never lost its appeal.

SERVES 4   **PREPARATION** 25 minutes   **COOKING** 45–55 minutes

Olive oil 4–5 tbsp
Onions 350g (12oz), peeled and sliced
Aubergines 2, cut into 5mm (¼in) slices lengthways
Courgettes 2, cut into 5mm (¼in) slices lengthways
Potatoes 450g (1lb), peeled and cut into 1cm (½in) slices
Plum tomatoes 225g (8oz), sliced
Salt and freshly ground black pepper

Mozzarella cheese 150g (5oz), sliced
Feta cheese 75g (3oz), crumbled
Dried mixed herbs 1 tsp
Butter 25g (1oz)
Plain flour 25g (1oz)
Milk 300ml (½ pint)
Egg 1, white only
Italian-style hard cheese 50g (2oz), grated
Mixed salad to serve (optional)

1 Preheat the oven to 190°C/170°fan/ Gas 5.
2 Heat 2 tablespoons of the olive oil in a frying pan, add the onions and cook for 5 minutes or until softened.
3 Heat a griddle or frying pan until hot and griddle the aubergine and courgette slices, in batches, until softened and browned.
4 Parboil the potato slices for 5 minutes, then drain well.
5 In a 2 litre (3½ pint) baking dish, layer the tomatoes, onions, courgettes, aubergines and potatoes, seasoning with salt and pepper. Scatter over the mozzarella and sprinkle with the feta and mixed herbs.

6 Melt the butter in a saucepan, stir in the flour and milk and bring to the boil, stirring continuously until smooth and thick. Remove from the heat and season to taste. Whisk the egg white until stiff, fold into the sauce and pour over the cheeses. Sprinkle with the grated hard cheese and bake for 30–40 minutes until golden brown.
7 Serve immediately, with a mixed salad, if you like.

TIP

If cooking for vegetarians, make sure the cheeses are suitable.

AIR FRYER

Step 3, air fry the vegetables at 180°C for 15 minutes, turning frequently.

Calories	Fibre	Salt	Sugar	Fat
640	7g	1.8g	14g	52g of which 19g is saturated

Veggie Burgers

In the 1970s, vegetarian food was often disappointingly dull, but by the 1980s, when these veggie burgers were created, things were slowly changing. These old-school veggie burgers are moist, rich, nutty, filling and much tastier than many of the imitation-meat burgers on sale today.

MAKES 8   **PREPARATION** 15 minutes   **COOKING** 20 minutes

Butter 25g (1oz)
Onion 1, peeled and chopped
Plain flour 1 tbsp
Milk 150ml (¼ pint)
Chopped mixed nuts 225g (8oz)
Soy sauce 1 tbsp
Tomato purée 1 tbsp

Fresh breadcrumbs 175g (6oz)
Egg 1, beaten
Freshly ground black pepper
Burger buns, lettuce leaves, tomato slices, red onion rings, cheese slices and tomato ketchup to serve (optional)

1 Preheat the grill to medium–hot.
2 Melt the butter in a saucepan and fry the onion until soft. Stir in the flour and cook for 2 minutes.
3 Gradually add the milk, stirring continuously, and bring to the boil. Simmer for 1–2 minutes, stirring until smooth and thick.
4 Add the nuts, soy sauce, tomato purée, breadcrumbs, egg and pepper and mix well.
5 Divide the mixture into eight and shape into patties.
6 Grill for 4 minutes, then turn over and grill for 4 minutes more.
7 Serve immediately on buns with lettuce, tomato, onion rings, cheese and ketchup, if you like.

TIPS
Use wholemeal breadcrumbs if you prefer. Buy ready-chopped nuts, or make your own mixture and chop them yourself.
The nut mixture is quite sticky, so lightly flour your hands to make shaping the burgers easier. You can shape the patties in advance and chill them until you're ready to cook.

AIR FRYER
Step 6, air fry at 180°C for 8 minutes, turning halfway through, until golden.

Calories	Fibre	Salt	Sugar	Fat
279	1.3g	0.6g	5g	18g of which 4.5g is saturated

Cod with Parsley Sauce

Cod has been a favourite fish in England for over a thousand years and – as long as it's fresh and not overcooked – this simple recipe shows how good the pearly flakes of fish can be.

SERVES 4   **PREPARATION** 5 minutes   **COOKING** 8–10 minutes

Vegetable oil 1 tbsp
Skinless cod fillets or loin 4 pieces
Butter 25g (1oz)
Plain flour 25g (1oz)
Milk 300ml (½ pint)

Salt and freshly ground black pepper
Finely chopped parsley 1–2 tbsp
Steamed new potatoes and mixed vegetables to serve (optional)

1 Heat the oil in a non-stick frying pan and fry the fish for 2–3 minutes, then turn over and cook for about 3 minutes or until the fish is opaque.
2 Meanwhile, melt the butter in a saucepan. Add the flour and cook over a low heat, stirring, for 2 minutes. Do not let the mixture brown.
3 Gradually stir in the milk and cook, stirring continuously, until the sauce comes to the boil and thickens. Lower the heat and simmer very gently for 3 minutes.
4 Season to taste with salt and pepper, then stir in the parsley. Serve the cod with the parsley sauce and steamed new potatoes and vegetables, if you like.

VARIATION
■ **Cod with Butter Sauce** Instead of steps 2 and 3, gently heat 75g (3oz) clarified butter (see page 24) in a pan until browned, then stir in a teaspoon of white wine vinegar or lemon juice.

Calories	Fibre	Salt	Sugar	Fat
232	0.5g	1g	3.5g	11g of which 5g is saturated

Finnan Haddock

Finnan haddock (or finnan haddie) comes from the village of Findon, near Aberdeen. Lightly salted, then smoked, it became better known after the railway linked Aberdeen to London in the 1840s. It's often served for breakfast, and is used in the traditional Scottish soup, Cullen skink, but here it makes a cosy supper dish.

SERVES 2   **PREPARATION** 10 minutes   **COOKING** 15 minutes

Finnan haddock fillets 2
Bay leaf 1
Freshly ground black pepper
Milk 300ml (½ pint)
Butter 25g (1oz)
Plain flour 25g (1oz)

Eggs 2, hardboiled, shelled and chopped
Chopped parsley 1 tbsp
Boiled potatoes and fresh watercress or wilted spinach to serve (optional)

1 Put the haddock, skin side down, in a large frying pan. Add the bay leaf, some black pepper and the milk. Bring to the boil, cover and then simmer gently for 10 minutes until tender.
2 Transfer the fish to a warmed serving plate, reserving the milk. Cover and keep warm.
3 Melt the butter in a saucepan. Add the flour and cook gently, stirring continuously for 1 minute. Remove from the heat and gradually stir in the reserved milk. Bring to the boil, stirring all the time, and then simmer for 2–3 minutes until thick and smooth. Add the eggs and parsley and stir through.
4 Serve the fish with the hot sauce, with potatoes and watercress or wilted spinach if you like.

TIP
If you can't find finnan haddock, you can use any undyed smoked haddock.

Calories	Fibre	Salt	Sugar	Fat
542	1g	3.5g	7g	23g of which 12g is saturated

Family Fish Pie

Often served on a Friday (unless you had a 'chippy tea'!), there are many variations on this family favourite – you can use different fish, add prawns or leave out the eggs. This really tasty version has a colourful topping with swede and Red Leicester cheese.

SERVES 4   **PREPARATION** 25 minutes   **COOKING** 30 minutes

Potatoes 350g (12oz), peeled and diced
Swede 225g (8oz), peeled and diced
Eggs 2
Butter 50g (2oz)
Plain flour 50g (2oz)
Milk 600ml (1 pint), plus extra for mashing
Smoked haddock 450g (1lb), skinned and cubed

Frozen peas 110g (4oz)
Sweetcorn 198g can, drained
Chopped parsley 1 tbsp
Salt and freshly ground black pepper
Red Leicester cheese 50g (2oz), grated

1 Put the potatoes and swede in a pan of cold water and bring to the boil, then simmer for 10–15 minutes until tender.
2 Meanwhile, cook the eggs until hardboiled, cool, then shell and chop.
3 Put the butter, flour and milk into a saucepan and bring to the boil, whisking continuously, until the sauce is smooth and thick.
4 Add the fish, peas and sweetcorn and cook for 2–5 minutes until the fish is just cooked. Stir in the eggs and parsley and transfer the mixture to a baking dish; keep warm.
5 Preheat the grill to hot.
6 Drain the potatoes and swede and mash with a little milk until smooth. Season to taste, then spoon over the fish mixture. Sprinkle with the cheese and place under the hot grill for a few minutes until the cheese has melted. Serve hot.

TIPS

Most supermarkets now sell fish pie mix which has smoked haddock, salmon and white fish and this could be used in place of the smoked haddock.
Replace the swede with sweet potato if you prefer.

Calories	Fibre	Salt	Sugar	Fat
569	6g	2.5g	14g	25g of which 14g is saturated

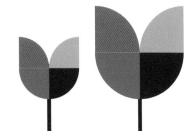

Scampi & Chips

Sophisticated pub grub in the 1970s meant scampi and chips 'in a basket'. You can do without the basket but don't forget the lemon wedges and a creamy lemon mayo dip.

SERVES 2   **PREPARATION** 20 minutes   **COOKING** 35–40 minutes

Baking potatoes 2, scrubbed
Groundnut or sunflower oil 2 tbsp
Salt and freshly ground black pepper
Dried white breadcrumbs 65g (2½oz)
Garlic granules ½ tsp
Melted butter 2 tbsp
Chopped fresh parsley 2 tbsp
Raw peeled jumbo king prawns 165g pack

Plain flour 2 tbsp, seasoned
Egg 1, beaten
Mayonnaise 2 tbsp
Greek-style yogurt 2 tbsp
Lemon 1, zest grated, then cut into wedges
Peas to serve (optional)

1 Preheat the oven to 220°C/200°fan/Gas 7. Cut the potatoes into 1cm (½in) slices then into 1cm (½in) chips. Scatter over a baking tray, toss with the oil and season. Bake for 35–40 minutes, turning halfway, until crisp and golden.
2 Meanwhile, line another baking tray with baking paper.
3 In a bowl, mix together the breadcrumbs, garlic granules, butter and parsley.
4 Dip the prawns in the flour, then in the egg and finally in the breadcrumb mixture, coating them evenly.
5 Place on the lined baking tray and bake for the last 10 minutes of the chips' cooking time.

6 Meanwhile, stir together the mayonnaise, yogurt and lemon zest; season to taste.
7 Serve the scampi and chips with lemon mayo and lemon wedges for squeezing over, and freshly cooked peas, if you like.

AIR FRYER

Step 1, spray the air fryer drawer with oil, then air fry the chips at 180°C for 20-30 minutes, until cooked and crisp.
Step 5, spray the air fryer drawer with oil, then air fry the prawns at 180°C for 7–10 minutes, until golden brown and cooked through.

Calories	Fibre	Salt	Sugar	Fat
833	6g	2.8g	5g	47g of which 16g is saturated

Chicken Curry

Curry has a surprisingly long history in Britain: employees of the East India Company introduced it in the early eighteenth century and it became even more popular in Victorian times. In 1861 Mrs Beeton noted that shop-bought curry powder was generally far superior to homemade.

SERVES 4 **PREPARATION** 15 minutes **COOKING** 55 minutes

Skinless and boneless chicken thighs 4
Plain flour 2 tbsp, seasoned
Salt and freshly ground black pepper
Olive or rapeseed oil 1 tbsp
Onion 1, peeled and chopped
Garlic 1 clove, peeled and finely chopped
Cooking apple 1, peeled and chopped
Curry powder 1 tbsp

Ground ginger ½ tsp
Ground cinnamon ½ tsp
Chicken stock 300ml (½ pint)
Fruit chutney 1 tbsp, plus extra to serve
Sultanas 15–25g (½–1oz) (optional)
Natural yogurt 3 tbsp
Basmati rice, poppadums and lemon wedges to serve (optional)

1 Coat the chicken in the seasoned flour.
2 Heat the oil in a large saucepan and fry the chicken for about 5 minutes until golden. Using a slotted spoon, remove from the pan and set aside.
3 Add the onion, garlic and apple to the pan and gently fry for a few minutes until softened.
4 Stir in the spices and some salt and pepper. Then pour in the stock, add the chutney and sultanas, if using, and bring to the boil.
5 Return the chicken to the pan, cover and simmer gently for about 35 minutes or until the chicken is tender.
6 Stir in the yogurt then serve with freshly cooked basmati rice, poppadums, chutney and lemon wedges, if using.

TIP
Serve on wraps or with naan bread instead of rice.

VARIATION
■ **Vegetable Curry** Omit the chicken and use prepared vegetables, such as butternut squash, green beans, broccoli and spinach. There's no need to fry the veg: add at an appropriate stage for their cooking time.

Calories	Fibre	Salt	Sugar	Fat
210	3g	1.4g	12g	5g of which 1g is saturated

Chicken Kiev

Chicken Kiev, now often named Chicken Kyiv out of respect for Ukraine, originated around the beginning of the twentieth century, when it was seen on the menus of smart restaurants. Reimagined as a ready-meal in the 1970s, it has been one of the UK's most popular retro dishes ever since.

SERVES 2   **PREPARATION** 20 minutes   **COOKING** 20–25 minutes

Skinless chicken breasts 2 small
Butter 25g (1oz), at room temperature
Garlic 1 clove, peeled and crushed
Chopped parsley 1 tbsp
Plain flour 1 tbsp

Grated Parmesan cheese 1 tbsp
Egg 1, beaten
Cornflakes 50g (2oz), finely crushed
Cherry tomatoes and peas to serve (optional)

1 Preheat the oven to 180°C/160°fan/Gas 4. Line a baking tray with baking paper.
2 Cut a small horizontal slit in each chicken breast to make a pocket. Mix together the butter, garlic and parsley. Push this mixture into the chicken pockets and secure with cocktail sticks.
3 In a shallow dish mix together the flour and Parmesan. Put the beaten egg in another dish and the cornflakes in another. Coat the chicken in the flour, then in the egg and finally the cornflakes.
4 Place on the baking tray and bake for 20–25 minutes until cooked through.
5 Remove the cocktail sticks and serve with cherry tomatoes and peas, or other vegetables of your choice.

TIP
Crush the cornflakes by putting them into a plastic bag and rolling with a rolling pin.

AIR FRYER
Step 4, air fry at 180°C for 20 minutes or until cooked through.

Calories	Fibre	Salt	Sugar	Fat
420	1.5g	0.9g	1g	17g of which 9g is saturated

Coq au Vin

A classic French dish that became a dinner party favourite in the 1970s. The wine makes it very aromatic, and it can be made in advance and gently reheated.

SERVES 4 **PREPARATION** 20 minutes **COOKING** 1½ hours

Chicken legs 6
Plain flour 2 tbsp, seasoned
Salt and freshly ground black pepper
Butter 25g (1oz)
Olive or rapeseed oil 1 tbsp
Onions 8 small or 10 **shallots**, peeled
Garlic 1 clove, peeled and chopped
Lean bacon 110g (4oz), chopped

Finely chopped parsley 2 tbsp, plus extra to serve
Bay leaf 1
Red wine 300ml (½ pint)
Chicken stock 300ml (½ pint)
Button mushrooms 110g (4oz), wiped
Mashed potatoes and green vegetables to serve

1 Toss the chicken in the seasoned flour.
2 Heat the butter and oil in a large saucepan. Add the chicken and gently fry for about 5 minutes on each side until golden. Using a slotted spoon, remove from the pan and set aside.
3 Add the onions or shallots, garlic and bacon to the pan and gently fry until pale golden.
4 Return the chicken to the pan with the parsley, bay leaf, wine and stock. Bring to the boil, then cover the pan and simmer gently for 45 minutes.
5 Add the mushrooms and simmer, uncovered, for a further 15 minutes.
6 Sprinkle with parsley and serve hot, with buttery mash and green vegetables.

TIPS
Choose a wine that you're happy to drink the rest of the bottle with your meal. You could use white wine instead of red.

Calories	Fibre	Salt	Sugar	Fat
548	5g	1.8g	10g	22g of which 10g is saturated

Leek & Bacon Stovies

A traditional Scottish potato-based dish, its name derives from the French word etuvé, meaning stewed or braised in a covered pot. There are almost as many recipes for this homely comfort food as there are cooks in Scotland.

SERVES 4   **PREPARATION** 20 minutes   **COOKING** 1 hour

Butter 25g (1oz)
Vegetable oil 1 tbsp
Smoked streaky bacon 4 rashers, chopped
Floury potatoes 680g (1½lb), peeled and diced
Carrot 1 large, peeled and finely chopped
Ground nutmeg pinch

Salt and freshly ground black pepper
Leek 1 large, trimmed and sliced
Beef, chicken or vegetable stock 150ml (¼ pint)
Chopped fresh parsley or chives 2 tbsp
Oatcakes or crusty bread to serve (optional)

1 Heat the butter and oil in a large saucepan and fry the bacon for 4–5 minutes until lightly browned.
2 Add the potatoes, carrot and nutmeg, season and mix well. Cover, reduce the heat to as low as possible and cook for 15 minutes.
3 Stir in the leek and stock and bring to the boil. Cover, reduce the heat to low and cook for 40 minutes or until the potatoes have collapsed.
4 Spoon into mugs or bowls and scatter with chopped herbs. Serve with oatcakes or crusty bread, if you like.

TIPS
The best stovies are made using floury potatoes such as King Edward or Maris Piper.
Traditionally the juices from the roast joint along with a little water were stirred into the potatoes to finish the cooking, but stock makes a good alternative.
You can add other root vegetables, such as sweet potato, parsnip, turnip and swede: cut into pieces the same thickness as the potato.
Leave out the bacon and use vegetable stock for a veggie version.

Calories	Fibre	Salt	Sugar	Fat
296	6g	2g	4g	14g of which 5g is saturated

Quiche Lorraine

Quiche Lorraine originated in eastern France in the early seventeenth century. It went on to become the ultimate 1970s buffet food. It's equally good served hot or cold.

SERVES 4-5 **PREPARATION** 30 minutes **COOKING** 1 hour

Plain flour 225g (8oz), plus extra for dusting
Salt ¼ tsp
Butter 110g (4oz), chilled and cubed
Streaky bacon 110g (4oz), cut into strips
Milk 150ml (¼ pint)

Single cream 150ml (¼ pint)
Eggs 3, beaten
Salt and freshly ground black pepper
Ground nutmeg large pinch
Green salad and tomatoes to serve (optional)

1 Preheat the oven to 200°C/180°fan/Gas 6.
2 Put the flour, salt and butter into a food processor and whizz until combined. Add cold water, 1 teaspoon at a time, and whizz until the pastry comes together.
3 Roll out the pastry on a floured work surface. Use to line a 20cm (8in) flan tin.
4 Put the bacon into a small non-stick frying pan and cook over a low heat until the bacon is soft but not crisp. Drain on kitchen paper, then place in the pastry case.
5 Heat the milk and cream to just below boiling point. Remove from the heat, add the eggs and lightly whisk to combine. Season to taste and add the nutmeg. Pour into the pastry case.
6 Bake for 10 minutes. Reduce the oven temperature to 170°C/150°fan/Gas 3 and bake for a further 35–45 minutes until set.
7 Leave to cool in the tin for 5–10 minutes before slicing. Serve with a green salad and tomatoes, if you like.

VARIATIONS

■ **Broccoli & Stilton Quiche** Instead of bacon, use 75g (3oz) blanched broccoli florets and 50g (2oz) crumbled Stilton.

■ **Leek & Cheese Quiche** Cook a sliced leek in a little butter until softened, then place in the pastry case and sprinkle over 50g (2oz) grated cheese.

Calories	Fibre	Salt	Sugar	Fat
530	2g	2.2g	2g	35g of which 19g is saturated

Crispy Pancakes

Since the well-known brand of crispy pancakes launched in 1958, generations of children looked forward to them when they came home from school. Try these for a retro dinner for friends and bring back the memories.

SERVES 4 **PREPARATION** 20 minutes **COOKING** 35 minutes

Grated mozzarella and cheese mix 110g (4oz)
Reduced fat soft cheese 75g (3oz)
Thick-cut roast ham 2 slices, finely chopped
Snipped chives 2 tbsp
Dijon mustard 1 tsp
Salt and freshly ground black pepper

Plain flour 110g (4oz)
Eggs 3
Milk 125ml (4½fl oz)
Olive oil spray for frying
Panko breadcrumbs 25g (1oz)
Paprika ¼ tsp
Salad to serve (optional)

1 Preheat the oven to 200°C/180°fan/ Gas 6. Line a baking tray with baking paper.

2 In a bowl mix together the grated cheese, soft cheese, ham, chives, mustard and some black pepper.

3 Sift the flour into another bowl and crack in two eggs. Whisk together, then gradually whisk in the milk to make a smooth thick batter.

4 Heat a frying pan and spray with a little oil. Pour in a quarter of the batter and swirl the pan to make a 16–18cm (approx. 7in) pancake. Cook for 1–2 minutes on each side until just cooked. Remove the pancake and repeat with the remaining batter.

5 Lay the pancakes on a board and divide the cheese mixture between them. Brush a little beaten egg around the edge of half of each pancake and fold over. Transfer to the baking tray and brush both sides with egg. Mix together the breadcrumbs and paprika and dust over the pancakes. Spray with a little oil.

6 Bake for 20 minutes until crisp and golden. Serve immediately, with salad if you like.

TIPS

If you don't have any olive oil spray, wipe the frying pan with kitchen paper soaked in a little oil; lightly drizzle the breadcrumbed pancakes with oil.
You can use almost any ready-cooked filling, such as a minced beef mixture, or chicken and sweetcorn, bacon and mushrooms, or fish in a white sauce.

AIR FRYER

Step 6, air fry at 180°C for 10 minutes or until hot and golden.

Calories	Fibre	Salt	Sugar	Fat
341	1.5g	1.2g	3g	16g of which 7g is saturated

Ham with Pease Pudding

One of Britain's oldest dishes, this began as pease pottage, later gaining the name it's known by now and popularised in the nursery rhyme Pease pudding hot, Pease pudding cold, Pease pudding in the pot, nine days old. We wouldn't recommend keeping it nine days – just cooked, with succulent ham, is perfect!

SERVES 4   **PREPARATION** 30 minutes plus soaking   **COOKING** 1¼ hours

Yellow split peas 450g (1lb), soaked overnight
Onion 1 large, peeled and chopped
Unsmoked streaky bacon 4 rashers, chopped
Salt and freshly ground black pepper
Unsmoked gammon joint 750g (1lb 10oz)
Bay leaves 2
Cloves 4
Cornflour 2 tbsp
Milk 300ml (½ pint)
Chopped parsley 2 tbsp, plus sprigs to garnish
Worcestershire sauce 1 tsp
Butter 15g (½oz)

1 Drain the peas and put them in a large saucepan. Add the onion, bacon, 2 teaspoons of salt and enough water to come at least 2.5cm (1in) above the peas. Bring to the boil and keep the water boiling rapidly for 10 minutes.
2 Lower the heat and simmer gently for about 50 minutes, stirring occasionally, until the peas are a purée and most of the liquid has been absorbed. Drain if necessary.
3 Meanwhile, bring a large pan of water to the boil, and add the gammon, bay leaves, cloves and 1 teaspoon of salt. Cover and simmer gently for 1 hour 10 minutes or until tender and cooked through.
4 Remove from the heat and leave to stand, covered, for 15 minutes. Drain the gammon, reserving the cooking liquid. Cover and keep warm. Discard the bay leaves and cloves.

5 In another pan, blend the cornflour with a little of the milk until smooth. Stir in the remaining milk and 300ml (½ pint) of the reserved stock. Heat, stirring, until the mixture boils, and then simmer for 1 minute until thickened. Remove from the heat, season to taste and stir in the chopped parsley. Keep warm.
6 To serve, add the Worcestershire sauce and butter to the pea mixture and adjust the seasoning if necessary. Cut the gammon into thick slices. Pile the pease pudding onto warmed serving plates and top with a few slices of gammon. Serve with the parsley sauce and a sprig of fresh parsley.

TIP

Traditionally, the peas were put into a pudding cloth and cooked in the water along with the meat. If preferred, you could cook the gammon joint first and use the cooking liquid to cook the peas.

Calories	Fibre	Salt	Sugar	Fat
836	10.5g	5.3g	8g	29g of which 11g is saturated

Toad-in-the-Hole

Batter puddings began to gain popularity in the early eighteenth century, but this British staple didn't get its name until later in the 1700s. Why the sausage is called the 'toad', no one knows! A filling family supper, traditionally served with onion gravy. This version has a tasty twist – a sage and onion topping.

SERVES 4   **PREPARATION** 15 minutes   **COOKING** 45–50 minutes

Vegetable oil 2 tbsp
Pork chipolatas 340g pack (12 sausages)
Plain flour 110g (4oz)
Eggs 2 medium
Semi-skimmed milk 300ml (½ pint)
Salt and freshly ground black pepper

Sage leaves 12 (optional)
Onion 1, peeled and sliced into thin rings (optional)
Steamed broccoli and gravy to serve (optional)

1 Preheat the oven to 220°C/200°fan/ Gas 7. Spoon 1 tablespoon of oil into a small roasting tin and put it in the oven while it heats up. When the oil is hot, add the sausages, shake the tin and cook for 15 minutes.
2 Meanwhile, put the flour, eggs and half the milk in a large jug. Use an electric whisk to make a thick bubbly batter. Stir in the remaining milk with plenty of salt and pepper.
3 Take the roasting tin out of the oven, then quickly pour the batter over the sausages. Cook for 30–35 minutes until puffed up and crisp.
4 Meanwhile, if making the sage and onion topping, heat the remaining oil in a frying pan, add the sage leaves and fry for 30–45 seconds. Using a slotted spoon, remove the leaves and set aside.

Add the onion rings to the pan, cover and cook over medium heat for 5 minutes, then uncover and cook until browned.
5 Scatter the onion and sage over the toad-in-the-hole and serve immediately, with broccoli and gravy, if you like.

TIP
Use vegetarian sausages if you prefer. Beef or venison sausages would be good too.

Calories	Fibre	Salt	Sugar	Fat
483	3.5g	1.7g	6g	31g of which 10g is saturated

Sausage & Leek Supper

This comforting family dish has been around since the sixties and is one of the most requested Dairy Diary recipes of all time, which definitely makes it a retro classic!

SERVES 6   **PREPARATION** 15 minutes   **COOKING** 35-45 minutes

Potatoes 700g (1lb 9oz), peeled and sliced
Butter 25g (1oz)
Sausages with herbs 450g (1lb), sliced
Onion 1, peeled and sliced
Leeks 4, trimmed and sliced
Plain flour 40g (1½oz)

Milk 450ml (¾ pint)
Smoked Cheddar cheese 110g (4oz), grated
Fresh breadcrumbs 25g (1oz)
Roast baby vegetables to serve (optional)

1 Preheat the oven to 200°C/180°fan/Gas 6.

2 Cook the potatoes in boiling salted water for 4-5 minutes until just tender. Drain.

3 Meanwhile, melt the butter in a large pan, add the sausage slices and cook for 5 minutes. Add the onion and leeks and cook for a further 5 minutes.

4 Add the flour, cook for 1 minute, then gradually add the milk and 75g (3oz) of the cheese, stirring. Bring to the boil then simmer for 1-2 minutes, stirring continuously.

5 Transfer to a 2 litre (3½ pint) baking dish and arrange the potato slices on top. Sprinkle with the breadcrumbs and the remaining cheese and bake for 20-30 minutes until browned.

6 Serve hot, with roast vegetables, if you like.

TIP

Keep an eye on the potato slices as you boil them; you want them to be only just tender as they will cook further when the dish goes into the oven. If overcooked they will be tricky to arrange on the top.

Calories	Fibre	Salt	Sugar	Fat
541	8g	1.4g	10g	32g of which 15g is saturated

Sausage & Pickle Pie

Branston pickle originates from the Staffordshire village of Branston and celebrated its 100th birthday in 2022. With 17 million jars sold annually, it's no wonder Branston pickle is familiar to most of us. This delicious pickle pie is perfect for a picnic or packed lunch, or warm with steamed vegetables.

SERVES 6   **PREPARATION** 25 minutes   **COOKING** 1 hour

Eggs 6 medium, at room temperature
Plain flour 1 tbsp, plus extra for dusting
Shortcrust pastry sheet 320g pack
Pork sausage meat 600g (1lb 5oz)

Branston pickle (sweet pickle) 6 tbsp
Beaten egg or milk to glaze
Steamed vegetables or salad to serve

1 Bring a pan of water to a simmer and carefully lower in the eggs, one at a time. Simmer for 8 minutes then drain and submerge in a bowl of cold water for 2 minutes. Peel away the shells. Roll the peeled eggs in the flour and set aside.
2 Preheat the oven to 200°C/180°fan/Gas 6.
3 On a lightly floured surface, roll out the pastry a little more and use to line a 23cm (9in) round deep pie dish.
4 Press half the sausage meat over the base of the pie then top with the boiled eggs. Dollop the pickle between the eggs. Press the remaining sausage meat over the eggs.

5 Re-roll the remaining pastry to make a lid for the pie, brush the edges with a little beaten egg or milk and lift over the pie filling. Press down the edges to seal and pinch all the way around. Cut out leaves from the pastry trimmings, if you like, then brush the top of the pie with egg or milk and decorate with the pastry leaves.
6 Bake for 20 minutes then reduce the oven temperature to 180°C/160°fan/Gas 4 and continue cooking for 30 minutes. Leave to cool for 30 minutes.
7 To serve, cut into six wedges and serve warm or cold, with steamed vegetables or salad.

Calories	Fibre	Salt	Sugar	Fat
690	5g	2.6g	10g	48g of which 17g is saturated

Liver & Bacon with Onion Gravy

Liver makes the best-tasting gravy ever! Serve this
old family favourite with mash and cabbage.

SERVES 4   **PREPARATION** 20 minutes   **COOKING** 20 minutes

Lambs' liver 450g (1lb)
Plain flour 2 tbsp, seasoned
Salt and white pepper
Sunflower oil 2 tbsp
Onion 1 large, peeled and sliced
Beef or lamb stock cube 1
Boiling water 500ml (18fl oz)

Instant beef gravy granules 1 tbsp
(optional)
Streaky bacon 8 rashers
**Mashed potato and cooked shredded
Savoy cabbage** (see Tip) to serve

1 Trim any sinews from the liver and slice
into bite-sized strips. Coat the liver in
seasoned flour.
2 Heat the oil in a large frying pan and
fry the onion until softened.
3 Add the liver to the pan and cook for 1
minute on each side.
4 Make up the stock with the boiling
water (see Tip). Pour over the liver, stir
well and bring to the boil, then lower the
heat and simmer uncovered for 5–8
minutes, stirring from time to time. If you
prefer thicker gravy, sprinkle with the
gravy granules and stir until the gravy
thickens.
5 Meanwhile, preheat the grill and grill
the bacon until crisp.
6 Serve the liver and onion gravy on
warmed serving plates and top each with
two rashers of bacon. Serve with plenty
of buttery mash and Savoy cabbage.

TIP
Use the liquid from boiling the cabbage
to make up the stock.

Calories	Fibre	Salt	Sugar	Fat
421	1.5g	3.4g	2g	25g of which Xg is saturated

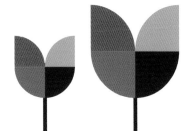

Roast Lamb with Fresh Mint Sauce

Roast leg of lamb makes a succulent Sunday lunch. Lamb has been paired with mint for over 200 years, so if you have some fresh mint to hand, try this traditional mint sauce.

SERVES 6   **PREPARATION** 20 minutes   **COOKING** 1¾ hours

Leg of lamb 2.2kg (4lb 12oz), at room temperature
Rosemary 15–20 small sprigs
Olive oil 1–2 tbsp
Salt and freshly ground black pepper
Plain flour 2 tbsp
Red or white wine 150ml (¼ pint)
Lamb or chicken stock 300ml (½ pint)
Roast potatoes and steamed leeks to serve

For the mint sauce
Mint leaves 50g (2oz)
Caster sugar 1½ tbsp
Boiling water 3 tbsp
White or red wine vinegar 150ml (¼ pint)

1 Preheat the oven to 220°C/200°fan/Gas 7. Using a small, sharp knife, make 15–20 incisions all over the lamb. Insert a sprig of rosemary into each incision. Put the lamb on a rack in a roasting tin, drizzle with olive oil and sprinkle with salt.
2 Roast the lamb for 20 minutes, then reduce the oven temperature to 180°C/160°fan/Gas 4. If you like your lamb slightly pink, continue cooking for another 1 hour 10 minutes. For well-done lamb, continue cooking for a further 10 minutes – but take care not to overcook.
3 While the lamb is cooking – about 20 minutes before the lamb is due to be ready – make the mint sauce. Put the mint leaves on a chopping board, sprinkle with the sugar and chop finely. Place in a bowl and stir in the boiling water, then stir in the vinegar. Pour into a serving jug or bowl.
4 Carefully transfer the leg of lamb to a serving dish, loosely cover with foil and set aside while you make the gravy.
5 To make the gravy, pour the cooking juices from the roasting tin into a bowl, and then skim off all the fat from the surface.
6 Pour 2–3 tablespoons of the lamb fat into the roasting tin and stir in the flour, then add the cooking juices, wine and stock. Bring to the boil over a medium heat, stirring and scraping any browned residue from the bottom of the tin. Leave to simmer gently for 10 minutes. Season to taste and then strain into a warmed gravy boat or jug.
7 Carve the lamb and serve with roast potatoes and sliced steamed leeks.

TIP

For a glossy finish, spread 2 tablespoons of honey over the lamb about 10 minutes before the end of cooking.

Calories	Fibre	Salt	Sugar	Fat
421	0.5g	0.8g	5g	17g of which 6g is saturated

Lancashire Hotpot

The topping of golden, crisp coins of potato makes this dish a northern classic. Some recipes use lamb chops, others omit the kidneys and add oysters, but the secret is always long, slow cooking.

SERVES 4–6   **PREPARATION** 25 minutes   **COOKING** 2½ hours

Diced lamb neck fillet 900g (2lb)
Plain flour 2 tbsp, seasoned
Salt and freshly ground black pepper
Butter 50g (2oz), melted, plus extra for greasing
Potatoes 900g (2lb), peeled and thinly sliced

Lambs' kidneys 3, cored and halved (optional)
Onions 3, peeled and thinly sliced
Mushrooms 225g (8oz), halved
Beef stock 600ml (1 pint)
Pickled red cabbage to serve (optional)

1 Preheat the oven to 170°C/150°fan/ Gas 3.
2 Coat the lamb in the seasoned flour.
3 Grease a deep casserole, then add a layer of potato slices and season with salt and pepper. Top with the lamb, kidneys (if using), onions and mushrooms. Season, then finish with a layer of potatoes.
4 Pour the stock over the potatoes, then brush with the melted butter. Cover the casserole and bake for 2 hours until the meat and potatoes are tender.
5 Turn the oven up to 220°C/200°fan/ Gas 7. Uncover the casserole and cook for a further 30 minutes until the potatoes are golden brown.
6 Serve hot, with red cabbage, if you like.

TIPS
You could use lamb chops or mutton, if you prefer.
Floury potatoes such as Maris Piper or King Edward work well in a hotpot, softening underneath and going crispy on top.

Calories	Fibre	Salt	Sugar	Fat
508	5.5g	1.4g	6g	20g of which 10g is saturated

Shepherd's Pie

The invention of the hand-cranked meat mincer in the mid-1800s helped cooks to make new meals out of leftover roast meat. Shepherd's pie has proved enduringly popular, whether it's made from leftover or fresh meat, and this version is absolutely delicious.

SERVES 4   **PREPARATION** 20 minutes   **COOKING** 55 minutes

Minced lamb 450g (1lb)
Onion 1, peeled and diced
Carrot 1 large, peeled and diced
Plain flour 1 tbsp
Lamb or vegetable stock 300ml (½ pint), hot
Bay leaf 1
Rosemary or thyme sprig or pinch of dried thyme or oregano
Salt and freshly ground black pepper

Worcestershire sauce 1 tbsp
Tomato purée 1 tbsp
Potatoes 900g (2lb), peeled and cut into chunks
Milk 150ml (¼ pint)
Butter 50g (2oz)
Leicester, Lancashire or Cheddar cheese 25g (1oz), grated
Cooked cabbage or broccoli to serve

1 Heat a frying pan over a high heat, add the lamb and dry fry for a few minutes, breaking it up with a wooden spoon until evenly browned. Add the onion and carrot and cook, stirring occasionally, for 5 minutes.
2 Sprinkle in the flour and cook for a minute then pour in the stock, add the herbs, salt, pepper, Worcestershire sauce and tomato purée. Simmer, uncovered, for 20–25 minutes until the sauce has thickened. Remove the bay leaf and herb sprigs.
3 Meanwhile, preheat the oven to 190°C/170°fan/Gas 5. Put a pie dish in the oven to heat up for 5 minutes.
4 Cook the potatoes in boiling salted water for about 15 minutes until tender. Drain well, then return the potatoes to the pan, over the heat, and let them dry out for half a minute. Add the milk and when it comes to the boil, take the pan

off the heat, add the butter and plenty of salt and pepper and mash the potatoes until smooth.
5 Spoon the mince mixture into the dish. Spoon the hot mash on top and carefully spread it all over the mince. Sprinkle with the cheese. Put the dish on a baking sheet and bake for 20–25 minutes until browned on top.
6 Serve hot, with freshly cooked cabbage or broccoli.

TIPS
Replace some of the potato with diced swede or butternut squash if you like. If you like a little crunch, top with panko breadcrumbs. You can speed up the cooking by grilling the pie for 5–8 minutes rather than baking it in the oven. For extra flavour you could add a can of chopped tomatoes, some crushed garlic or a pinch of cayenne pepper.

Calories	Fibre	Salt	Sugar	Fat
614	7g	1.4g	9g	30g of which 16g is saturated

Corned Beef Hash

Hash comes from the French word hacher, to chop up, and the French dish Hachis Parmentier is similar to our shepherd's pie. Corned beef began to be imported from Uruguay in the 1860s, and is still a great stand-by ingredient for this tasty lunch or supper dish.

SERVES 4   **PREPARATION** 15 minutes   **COOKING** 20 minutes

Potatoes 450g (1lb), peeled and cubed
Salt and freshly ground black pepper
Olive or rapeseed oil 2 tbsp
Spring onions 4, finely chopped
Garlic 1 clove, crushed

Red chilli 1, deseeded and finely sliced
Cabbage 110g (4oz), finely shredded
Corned beef 350g (12oz), chopped
Finely chopped parsley 2 tbsp
Eggs 4

1 Put the potatoes in a saucepan of lightly salted water and bring to the boil, then simmer for 5 minutes. Drain well.
2 Heat the oil in a large frying pan and fry the potatoes for 4–5 minutes until lightly golden.
3 Add the spring onions, garlic, chilli and cabbage and stir-fry for 3–4 minutes.
4 Stir in the corned beef and use a fork to lightly crush with the potatoes. Stir in the parsley and season to taste.
5 Meanwhile, poach the eggs: break each egg into a cup and bring a pan of water to the boil. Using a spoon, swirl the water then slide an egg into the centre and cook for 2–3 minutes. Using a slotted spoon, carefully lift out and repeat with the remaining eggs.
6 Spoon the hash onto warmed plates and top with the poached eggs.

TIP
Use leftover roast beef, lamb or duck instead of the corned beef.

Calories	Fibre	Salt	Sugar	Fat
414	4g	2.6g	3g	21g of which 7g is saturated

Farmhouse Mince

An easy one-pan dish that's been popular since the sixties. This gently spiced family supper can easily be tweaked to use the spices in your cupboard.

SERVES 4–6　**PREPARATION** 10 minutes　**COOKING** 50 minutes

Lean minced beef 500g (1lb 2oz)
Onion 1, peeled and chopped
Red lentils 50g (2oz), rinsed
Tomato purée 1 tbsp
Paprika 1 tsp
Cayenne pepper 1 tsp

Worcestershire sauce 1 tbsp
Beef stock 600ml (1 pint)
Salt and freshly ground black pepper
Frozen mixed vegetables 200g (7oz)
Mashed potato to serve (optional)

1 Heat a large non-stick saucepan over a high heat, add the minced beef and onion and dry fry for about 5 minutes until the beef has browned.
2 Add the lentils, tomato purée, spices, Worcestershire sauce and beef stock, and season to taste. Bring to the boil, then cover and simmer for 40 minutes, stirring occasionally.
3 Add the vegetables to the pan, cover and simmer for a further 5 minutes, or until the vegetables are tender.
4 Serve with mash, if you like.

TIPS
Omit the paprika and cayenne and use curry powder and turmeric or garam masala, if you like.
Instead of mash, serve with naan breads and/or freshly cooked rice.

Calories	Fibre	Salt	Sugar	Fat
184	1.8g	1.1g	4g	5g of which 2g is saturated

Mince & Onion Pie

Pie & mash has been a classic since Victorian times and was popularised in the Docklands area of London, often served with a parsley sauce or jellied eels. For most, it is now more likely to be served with gravy, or with mushy peas if you're 'up north'. Pies come with an endless variety of fillings; here we share the ever-popular mince & onion.

SERVES 6 **PREPARATION** 30 minutes **COOKING** 1¼ hours

Lean minced beef 500g (1lb 2oz)
Onion 1 large, peeled and chopped
Carrots 200g (7oz), peeled and diced
Worcestershire sauce 1 tbsp
Beef stock 500ml (18fl oz)
Tomato ketchup 2 tbsp

Freshly ground black pepper
Instant beef gravy granules 2 tbsp
Plain flour for dusting
Puff pastry sheet 320g pack
Beaten egg or milk to glaze
Mashed potato, peas and gravy to serve

1 Heat a non-stick heavy-based frying pan over a high heat, add the mince and dry fry, stirring constantly, until evenly browned.

2 Add the onion and carrots, Worcestershire sauce, beef stock and ketchup and season with pepper. Stir well and bring to the boil, then cover and simmer for 20 minutes. Remove the lid and allow to bubble for a further 15 minutes.

3 Sprinkle the gravy granules over and stir until the liquid thickens. Leave to cool completely.

4 When ready to cook, preheat the oven to 200°C/180°fan/Gas 6.

5 On a lightly floured surface, roll out the pastry a little more then cut a 2.5cm (1in) strip long enough to go around the edge of a 700ml (1¼ pint) pie dish and a pastry lid slightly larger than the dish.

Brush the rim of the dish with beaten egg or milk and press the pastry strip onto the rim.

6 Spoon the cooled mince into the dish. Lift the pastry lid over the filling, pressing the edges down well to seal. Trim and crimp the edges all the way around. Re-roll the pastry trimmings and cut out leaves to decorate the top of the pie. Brush the top with beaten egg or milk and bake for 30–35 minutes until the pastry is risen and deep golden.

7 Serve hot with mash, peas and gravy.

TIP

If time allows, make the mince the night before so it has time to cool down. If you use it when it's hot, the mince will make the pastry sweat.

Calories	Fibre	Salt	Sugar	Fat
374	4g	1.8g	7g	19g of which 9g is saturated

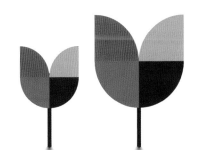

Teviotdale Pie

Teviotdale is a valley in the Scottish Borders, near the town of Hawick. This minced beef pie from the region has a deep, pillowy suet crust. A generous pile of buttered cabbage, green beans or broccoli would be the perfect accompaniment.

SERVES 4   **PREPARATION** 15 minutes   **COOKING** 1 hour

Lean minced beef 450g (1lb)
Onion 1, peeled and chopped
Carrot 1 large, peeled and finely chopped
Celery 2 sticks, finely chopped
Beef stock 300ml (½ pint)
Worcestershire sauce 1 tsp

Salt and freshly ground black pepper
Self-raising flour 225g (8oz)
Cornflour 25g (1oz)
Shredded suet 75g (3oz)
Milk 300ml (½ pint)
Steamed green vegetables to serve

1 Preheat the oven to 190°C/170°fan/Gas 5. Dry fry the meat in a large saucepan for about 5 minutes until it starts to brown. Add the onion, carrot and celery and cook for a further 5 minutes.

2 Pour the stock into the pan and add the Worcestershire sauce. Season to taste and simmer for 15 minutes until the vegetables are just tender.

3 Meanwhile, put the flour, cornflour and suet in a mixing bowl and gradually add the milk, stirring well, to form a thick batter. Season well.

4 Put the meat and vegetables in a 1.2 litre (2 pint) pie dish and cover with the batter. Put the dish on a baking sheet and cook for about 35 minutes until the topping is risen, crusty and browned.

5 Serve with freshly cooked green vegetables.

TIP
To freeze, leave to cool completely, wrap and freeze for up to 3 months. Defrost in the fridge overnight. Reheat, covered with foil, for 25–30 minutes at 180°C/160°fan/Gas 4, removing the foil for the last 5 minutes.

Calories	Fibre	Salt	Sugar	Fat
601	4.5g	1.8g	8g	25g of which 13g is saturated

Lobby

Lobby is the word used in Stoke-on-Trent for a beef stew. It may have originated from lobscouse, a stew from Liverpool, but many 'Stokies' believe it's so-called because you just 'lob' any vegetables in that need using up. The letters of lobby also come from: Left Over Bits and Bobs from Yesterday.

SERVES 4-6 **PREPARATION** 15 minutes **COOKING** 40 minutes Ⓕ

Potatoes 4, peeled and diced
Carrots 4, peeled and diced
Swede 1 small, peeled and diced
Onions 2, peeled and diced
Beef stock 1 litre (1¾ pints)
Stewing steak 395g can

Salt and freshly ground black pepper
Crusty bread or Yorkshire pudding to serve (optional)
Peas, cabbage or broccoli to serve (optional)

1 Put the vegetables in a large saucepan and pour in the stock. Bring to the boil, then simmer for 30 minutes or until soft.
2 Add the stewing steak and stir, breaking up the chunks of meat. Simmer for a further 5 minutes or until the steak is heated through.
3 Season to taste then serve with crusty bread or in a large Yorkshire pudding, with some cooked green vegetables if you like.

TIP
In Step 1, simmer 50g (2oz) pearl barley with the stock for 20 minutes before adding the vegetables, if you like.

Calories	Fibre	Salt	Sugar	Fat
209	6g	1.7g	10g	5g of which 2g is saturated

Beef Stroganoff

Sautéed beef with mustard and sour cream is a version of an old Russian dish; it first became popular when it was served by the chefs of Count Paul Stroganoff, a nineteenth-century celebrity. It made its way to restaurant menus, and by the 1960s had become a dinner party favourite.

SERVES 4   **PREPARATION** 10 minutes   **COOKING** 15 minutes

Butter 25g (1oz)
Rump steak 450g (1lb), trimmed and cut into strips
Onion 1, peeled and thinly sliced
Button mushrooms 110g (4oz), sliced
Dijon mustard 2 tsp
Soured cream 150ml (¼ pint)

Salt and freshly ground black pepper
Lemon juice 1 tsp
Paprika for dusting
Chopped parsley 2 tbsp
Cooked rice and lemon wedges to serve (optional)

1 Heat the butter in a frying pan over a high heat and fry the meat until browned. Using a slotted spoon, remove from the pan and set aside.
2 Add the onion and mushrooms to the pan and fry for about 5 minutes or until softened.
3 Stir in the mustard, then gradually stir in the soured cream.
4 Return the meat to the pan and gently reheat for 5 minutes. Season to taste and add the lemon juice. Dust with paprika and sprinkle with parsley.
5 Serve immediately, with rice and lemon wedges, if you like.

TIP
For a decadent open steak sandwich you could spoon the Stroganoff onto lightly toasted sliced sourdough bread and top with rocket or watercress.

Calories	Fibre	Salt	Sugar	Fat
333	1.5g	1.2g	3.5g	23g of which 13g is saturated

Steak & Kidney Pudding

England was known for its puddings, both sweet and savoury, since the seventeenth century, although the combination of steak and kidney first appeared in print in Mrs Beeton's Book of Household Management in 1861. Suet pastry became much easier to make after 1893, when Gabriel Hugon set up the first factory to produce shredded suet.

SERVES 4   **PREPARATION** 35 minutes   **COOKING** 3½–4 hours

Butter for greasing
Self-raising flour 225g (8oz), plus extra for dusting
Salt and freshly ground black pepper
Shredded suet 110g (4oz)
Stewing steak 450g (1lb), trimmed and cubed

Lambs' kidneys 175g (6oz), chopped
Plain flour 1 tbsp, seasoned
Onion 1 large, peeled and chopped
Steamed or boiled potatoes and green vegetables to serve

1 Grease a 900ml (1½ pint) pudding basin.
2 Sift the flour and ½ teaspoon of salt into a bowl and mix in the suet. Add 150ml (¼ pint) of cold water and mix to a soft dough.
3 On a lightly floured surface, roll out two-thirds of the dough and use to line the pudding basin.
4 Toss the steak and kidneys in the seasoned flour. Layer in the basin with the onion and add 300ml (½ pint) of water.
5 Roll out the remaining dough to make a lid. Moisten the edges of the dough in the basin with water, then cover with the lid and press the edges together to seal.
6 Cover with a double thickness of buttered greaseproof paper or single thickness of greased foil, making a pleat to allow the pudding to rise. Secure with string. Use extra string to make a handle for ease of removal.

7 Place in a steamer over a pan of hot water. Alternatively, place a metal trivet in a large saucepan, add the pudding and add boiling water to come halfway up the sides of the basin. Cover the pan and steam steadily for 3½–4 hours. Top up with more boiling water as necessary.
8 Serve hot, with potatoes and green vegetables.

TIPS
Beef suet or vegetable suet work equally well.
To reduce the steaming time, cook the filling before making the pastry. Heat 25g (1oz) butter and 1 tablespoon vegetable oil in a large saucepan, add the onion and fry for 5 minutes until softened, then add the steak and kidneys tossed in seasoned flour and fry, stirring once or twice, until browned. Set aside while you make the pastry. Assemble as above and steam for 2 hours.

Calories	Fibre	Salt	Sugar	Fat
662	3.5g	1.6g	2.5g	31g of which 17g is saturated

Steak Diane

Said to have been invented in a smart London restaurant in the 1930s, when it was cooked at the table, Steak Diane reappeared as a classic seventies' dinner party dish and is now usually served as a romantic dinner for two – serve with chunky chips and watercress for authenticity.

SERVES 2 **PREPARATION** 15 minutes
COOKING 10–20 minutes depending on how you like your steak cooked

Fillet steaks 2 (approx. 175g/6oz each)
Salt flakes and freshly ground black pepper
Butter 25g (1oz)
Sunflower oil 1 tbsp
Thyme 2 sprigs
Banana shallots 2, peeled and finely chopped
White button mushrooms 150g (5oz) sliced

Brandy 4 tbsp
Worcestershire sauce 1 tsp
Dijon mustard 1 tsp
Beef stock 300ml (½ pint)
Double cream 100ml (3½fl oz)
Finely chopped fresh tarragon 1 tbsp (optional)
Freshly cooked chips and watercress to serve

1 Put the steaks on a board and pat down with your hands, then season with salt and pepper. In a large heavy-based frying pan, heat the butter and oil together until bubbling, then add the steaks and thyme sprigs and fry for 3 minutes per side for rare, 4 minutes per side for medium rare, 5 minutes per side for medium or 6 minutes per side for well done.

2 Remove the steaks from the pan, loosely cover with foil and set aside.

3 Add the shallots and mushrooms to the pan and cook, stirring, until softened.

4 Tilt the pan away from you and add the brandy: if you have a gas hob it will ignite; if not, ignite with a match. Be very careful and protect yourself with an oven glove. When the flames have died down add the Worcestershire sauce, mustard and stock and bubble for 2 minutes.

5 Stir in the cream until you have a velvety mushroom sauce. Stir in the tarragon, if using.

6 Transfer the rested steaks to warmed serving plates. Spoon some of the sauce over each steak and serve with chips and watercress.

TIP
We use fillet steak but you can use sirloin if preferred.

Calories	Fibre	Salt	Sugar	Fat
716	2g	2g	5g	51g of which 27g is saturated

Puddings

95   TUTTI FRUTTI ICE CREAM
96   ARCTIC ROLL
     (ALSO CHOCOLATE ICE CREAM ROLL)
99   BLANCMANGE
100 BUTTERSCOTCH DELIGHT
103 FRUIT PAVLOVA
104 SUMMER PUDDING
     (ALSO AUTUMN PUDDING)
107 STRAWBERRY TRIFLE
     (ALSO PEAR & GINGER TRIFLE,
     BLACK FOREST TRIFLE,
     RASPBERRY & AMARETTI TRIFLE)
108 CHOCOLATE BAR CHEESECAKE
111 BLACK FOREST GATEAU
112 LEMON MERINGUE PIE
115 COCONUT JAM SPONGE PUDDING
116 EVE'S PUDDING
119 PINEAPPLE UPSIDE DOWN PUDDING
     (ALSO CHOCOLATE UPSIDE
     DOWN PUDDING)

120 SYRUP SPONGE PUDDING
     (ALSO CHOCOLATE SPONGE PUDDING,
     FRUIT SPONGE PUDDING,
     JAM SPONGE PUDDING)
123 JAM ROLY POLY
     (ALSO SYRUP ROLY POLY,
     LEMON ROLY POLY,
     MINCEMEAT ROLY POLY,
     SPOTTED DICK OR DOG)
124 CHOCOLATE PUDDING
127 SCHOOL CHOCOLATE
     CRACKNEL WITH PINK,
     GREEN OR CHOCOLATE CUSTARD
128 RICE PUDDING
     (ALSO TAPIOCA PUDDING,
     SEMOLINA PUDDING,
     SAGO PUDDING)
131 BAKED CUSTARDS
132 BREAD & BUTTER PUDDING
     (ALSO OSBORNE PUDDING)
135 FRUIT CRUMBLE
136 BUTTERSCOTCH APPLE PIE
139 TREACLE TART

Tutti Frutti Ice Cream

A nostalgic reminder of those wonderful seaside ice cream parlours (some of which are returning to coastal towns). Studded with colourful fruits, this easy-to-make ice cream gets its name from the Italian for 'all fruits' – tutti i frutti. Serve in a cone or in a dish with fan wafers.

SERVES 8   **PREPARATION** 10 minutes plus freezing

Whipping cream 600ml (1 pint)
Vanilla extract 1 tsp
Condensed milk 397g can

Glacé cherries 110g (4oz), quartered
Candied fruits or dried tropical fruits 225g (8oz), chopped

1 In a large bowl whip the cream to soft peaks with the vanilla.
2 Fold in the condensed milk and fruits.
3 Either pour into an ice cream maker and churn until frozen or pour into a container and freeze for at least 6 hours, stirring after 2–3 hours to distribute the fruit.

TIP
You could also include some chopped dried apricots, 2–3 pieces of chopped stem ginger or 50g (2oz) chopped pistachio nuts.

Calories	Fibre	Salt	Sugar	Fat
557	1g	0.2g	47g	34g of which 21g is saturated

Arctic Roll

Invented in the 1950s, this innovative dessert came onto the market in 1968, selling over 25 miles of frozen sponge pud every month in its heyday! Surprisingly easy to make, this homemade Arctic roll is much better than any mass-produced version.

SERVES 8-10   **PREPARATION** 25 minutes plus freezing   **COOKING** 10-12 minutes

Vanilla ice cream 400g (14oz)
Eggs 3
Caster sugar 75g (3oz)

Self-raising flour 75g (3oz)
Strawberry jam 4 tbsp, warmed
Icing sugar for sifting

1 Lay out a large sheet of baking paper and spoon the ice cream along the middle of the paper to form a sausage shape 30cm (12in) long. Roll the paper around the ice cream and twist the ends together. Freeze for 1 hour.

2 Preheat the oven to 200°C/180°fan/ Gas 6. Grease and line a 30 x 20cm (12 x 8in) Swiss roll tin.

3 In a large bowl, using an electric whisk, whisk the eggs for 2 minutes.

4 Add the sugar and continue whisking for a further 8-10 minutes until the mixture is very pale and thick – the consistency of softly whipped cream – and at least double its original volume.

5 Gently fold in the flour then spread in the prepared Swiss roll tin. Bake for 10-12 minutes until well risen and firm.

6 Turn out onto a fresh sheet of baking paper. Carefully peel off the lining paper and cut away any crisp edges with a sharp knife.

7 Leave to cool slightly, then spread with the jam. Unwrap the ice cream and place on the sponge, roll up tightly and hold in position for 1 minute. Re-wrap and freeze until ready to serve.

8 Sift a little icing sugar over the top before serving.

TIP
Use raspberry or cherry jam, lemon curd or toffee sauce instead of strawberry jam if you prefer.

VARIATION
■ **Chocolate Ice Cream Roll** Use 65g (2½oz) flour sifted twice with 15g (½oz) cocoa powder for the sponge. Fill with chocolate sauce and chocolate ice cream.

Calories	Fibre	Salt	Sugar	Fat
178	0.4g	0.2g	24g	5g of which 2.5g is saturated

Blancmange

Blancmange was originally a savoury dish; by the eighteenth century it had become a delicate dessert. The Victorian invention of 'blancmange powder' (flavoured cornflour) made the cook's task simpler, though the blancmange was often set in elaborate moulds. By the 1970s many birthday parties would include a blancmange made in a rabbit mould and sat upon green coconut or jelly 'grass'.

SERVES 4-6   **PREPARATION** 5 minutes plus setting   **COOKING** 10 minutes

Cornflour 4 tbsp
Milk 600ml (1 pint)
Vanilla extract 1 tsp
Caster sugar 3 tbsp
Butter 15g (½oz)

1 Blend the cornflour to a smooth paste with 3 tablespoons of the milk.
2 In a saucepan, warm the remaining milk then stir into the cornflour paste. Return to the pan and bring to the boil, stirring all the time, until the mixture thickens. Continue cooking for a further 3 minutes, stirring frequently.
3 Stir in the vanilla, sugar and butter.
4 Pour into a 600ml (1 pint) dampened jelly mould and leave in a cool place for several hours until set.
5 If you are using a rabbit jelly mould, you could make coconut 'grass': put the coconut in a small bowl, sprinkle over the green food colouring and stir until evenly coloured.
6 Turn the blancmange out onto a plate. Sprinkle the coconut grass around and add some sugar flowers, if you like. Alternatively, serve with fresh fruit.

To serve (optional)
Desiccated coconut 2-3 tbsp
Green food colouring 1 tsp
Sugar flowers or **fresh fruit**

VARIATIONS
■ **Chocolate Blancmange** Omit the vanilla and add 50g (2oz) melted chocolate.

■ **Coffee Blancmange** Omit the vanilla and add 1–2 tablespoons of coffee essence.

■ **Orange or Lemon Blancmange** Omit the vanilla and add 1 teaspoon of grated orange or lemon zest.

■ **Honey Blancmange** Use 1 tablespoon of honey instead of the caster sugar.

Calories	Fibre	Salt	Sugar	Fat
192	0g	0.1g	14g	6g of which 3.5g is saturated

Butterscotch Delight

Inspired by the instant powdered dessert launched by Bird's in 1967, which became ubiquitous during the seventies, this is a 'truly scrumptious' pud.

SERVES 4   **PREPARATION** 10 minutes plus cooling and chilling
COOKING 8 minutes   Ⓥ

Double cream 300ml (½ pint)
Unsalted butter 40g (1½oz), cubed
Soft light brown sugar 75g (3oz)

Vanilla extract ½ tsp
Glacé cherries 2, halved, to decorate (optional)

1 In a pan, gently heat 150ml (¼ pint) of the cream with the butter and sugar until the butter has melted and the sugar has dissolved.
2 Bring to the boil, then boil for 2 minutes until the mixture has thickened. Leave to cool, then chill for 1 hour.
3 Stir in the remaining cream and the vanilla extract, then whip the mixture until soft peaks form.
4 Spoon into four serving glasses, top with half a cherry, if using, and chill for 1 hour before serving.

TIPS
Best served on the same day as it's made. Instead of glacé cherries, serve with a few raspberries if you like.

Calories	Fibre	Salt	Sugar	Fat
518	0g	0.2g	19g	48g of which 30g is saturated

Fruit Pavlova

Originating in either Australia or New Zealand, this decadent dessert is named in honour of the Russian ballerina Anna Pavlova, who toured both countries in the 1920s. The crisp meringue with a marshmallowy centre is topped with whipped cream and fresh fruit; it looks spectacular and it's been a stylish dinner party centrepiece since the 1980s.

SERVES 8   **PREPARATION** 20 minutes   **COOKING** 1½ hours

Eggs 5, whites only
Caster sugar 300g (11oz)
White wine vinegar 1 tsp
Cornflour 1 tsp
Vanilla extract 1 tsp

Double cream 300ml (½ pint)
Ready-made custard 150g (5oz)
Selection of fresh fruit such as blueberries, raspberries and strawberries 500g (1lb 2oz)

1 Preheat the oven to 140°C/120°fan/ Gas 1 and line a large baking sheet with baking paper. Draw a circle about the size of a large dinner plate on the paper, then turn it over: you should still be able to see the circle.
2 In a large, grease-free mixing bowl whisk the egg whites until stiff. Gradually whisk in the sugar, 2 tablespoons at a time, until thick and glossy. Whisk in the vinegar, cornflour and vanilla.
3 Spoon the mixture onto the baking sheet and spread to fill the marked circle, making a slight dip in the centre.
4 Bake for 1½ hours, then turn off the oven and leave the meringue to cool in the oven.
5 Slide a palette knife under the meringue and transfer to a serving plate.
6 Whip the cream until soft peaks form, then whisk in the custard. Spoon onto the meringue. Top with fresh fruit and serve immediately.

TIP
Use any fruit you like, such as kiwifruit, peaches, mango or pineapple.

Calories	Fibre	Salt	Sugar	Fat
382	2g	0.1g	44g	21g of which 13g is saturated

Summer Pudding

Summer pudding is a perfect make-ahead dessert and a simple way to showcase summer fruits and use up bread that's a day or two old.

SERVES 4-6 **PREPARATION** 25 minutes plus chilling **COOKING** 7-10 minutes

White bread 9 large slices, crusts removed
Caster sugar 110g (4oz)
Soft summer fruit such as rhubarb, raspberries, strawberries, gooseberries,

stoned cherries, black or redcurrants, or a mixture of fruits 680g (1½lb), plus extra to decorate
Pouring cream to serve (optional)

1 Cut the bread into neat fingers.
2 Put the sugar and 5 tablespoons of water into a saucepan and heat slowly, stirring occasionally, until the sugar has dissolved. Add the fruit and simmer gently for about 7-10 minutes until starting to release their juices (gooseberries and blackcurrants may take a few minutes longer). Reserve a few spoonfuls of the juice.
3 Line the base and sides of a 1.2 litre (2 pint) pudding basin with bread fingers. Add half the hot fruit mixture. Cover with more bread fingers.
4 Pour in the remaining fruit mixture and top with the remaining bread fingers. Trim any excess bread. Cover with a saucer or plate and place a heavy weight, such as a can of tomatoes, on top. Chill overnight.
5 Turn out onto a serving plate. Spoon the reserved juice over the bread to cover any white patches. Decorate with fruit and serve with cream, if you like.

TIP
Use Madeira cake instead of bread if you like.

VARIATION
■ **Autumn Pudding** In place of summer fruit, use 680g (1½lb) prepared mixed autumn fruit such as chopped apples, pears, plums and blackberries; apples and pears may take 10-15 minutes to soften, but don't let them turn mushy.

Calories	Fibre	Salt	Sugar	Fat
202	5g	0.4g	26g	1g of which 0.2g is saturated

Strawberry Trifle

A fool-like 'trifle' appeared in a cookery book in 1585, but the dessert we know and love, combining cake, booze, fruit (or jelly), custard and cream has been popular ever since Hannah Glasse published her recipe for 'A Grand Trifle' in 1760.

SERVES 6   **PREPARATION** 25 minutes plus chilling

Trifle sponges 4 (approx. 110g/4oz), broken into pieces
Strawberries 350g (12oz), sliced
Caster sugar 2 tbsp
Sherry or marsala 2–4 tbsp

Reduced fat custard 425g can
Double cream 200ml (7fl oz)
Low fat natural yogurt 150g (5oz)
Colourful sprinkles to decorate

1 Arrange the trifle sponges in a single layer in a 1.2 litre (2 pint) glass dish. Place the strawberries on top and then sprinkle with sugar. Spoon the sherry or marsala over the strawberries.
2 Spoon the custard over the fruit and spread evenly.
3 Whip the cream until it just forms soft swirls then fold in the yogurt. Spoon over the custard and chill until required.
4 Decorate with sprinkles and serve.

TIPS
Decorate with sliced strawberries or shaved chocolate if you prefer.
Omit the yogurt and use more whipped cream.
You could sandwich the trifle sponges together with raspberry jam before cutting them into pieces.

VARIATIONS
■ **Pear & Ginger Trifle** Replace the sponge with ginger cake and the strawberries with drained canned pears. Omit the sugar.

■ **Black Forest Trifle** Replace the sponge with chocolate muffins and the strawberries with canned cherry pie filling. Omit the sugar.

■ **Raspberry & Amaretti Trifle** Sprinkle the sponges with crushed amaretti biscuits and replace the strawberries with raspberries.

Calories	Fibre	Salt	Sugar	Fat
362	2.5g	0.2g	26g	21g of which 13g is saturated

Chocolate Bar Cheesecake

This crowd-pleasing no-bake cheesecake would originally have been made using Marathon bars, which are now named Snickers. Several confectionary items, including Opal Fruits, changed their name and others, such as Pacer Mints, Toffo and Spangles disappeared from the shelves.

SERVES 8   **PREPARATION** 20 minutes plus chilling

Digestive biscuits 225g (8oz), crushed
Butter 75g (3oz), melted
Powdered gelatine 1 x 12g sachet
Full fat soft cheese 250g (9oz)
Icing sugar 50g (2oz)
Smooth peanut butter 50g (2oz)
Vanilla extract 1 tsp

Double cream 150ml (¼ pint), whipped
Snickers or other chocolate bars 5, roughly chopped
Salted caramel sauce for drizzling (optional)

1 Line a 20cm (8in) round loose-bottomed tin with a disc of baking paper. Mix the crushed biscuits with the butter and press into the tin.
2 Put 4 tablespoons of cold water in a small bowl, sprinkle over the gelatine and leave for 10 minutes. Place the bowl over a pan of hot water and stir until the gelatine has dissolved.
3 In a large bowl, beat together the soft cheese, icing sugar, peanut butter and vanilla. Fold in the gelatine, whipped cream and four chopped chocolate bars. Spoon into the lined tin and chill for at least 4 hours until firm.
4 To serve, remove from the tin, drizzle with caramel sauce, if using, and pile the remaining Snickers pieces in the centre.

TIP
If you're not keen on Snickers, try this with Fudge bars, Bounty bars or lightly crushed Maltesers.

Calories	Fibre	Salt	Sugar	Fat
676	2.5g	0.8g	29g	52g of which 27g is saturated

Black Forest Gateau

Black Forest gateau was a favourite restaurant dessert in the 1970s and 80s. This chocolate cake laced with kirsch, layered with whipped cream and cherries and topped with chocolate curls is a real treat to share with chocolate-loving friends and family.

SERVES 8–10   **PREPARATION** 50 minutes   **COOKING** 25 minutes

Butter 150g (5oz), plus extra for greasing
Plain flour 50g (2oz), sifted twice, plus extra for dusting
Eggs 6
Vanilla extract ½ tsp
Caster sugar 225g (8oz)
Cocoa powder 50g (2oz), sifted

Kirsch 4 tbsp
Double cream 450ml (¾ pint)
Black cherry pie filling 410g can
Chocolate curls (made with a vegetable peeler)

1 Preheat the oven to 180°C/160°fan/ Gas 4. Grease and flour the bases and sides of three 20cm (8in) sandwich tins.
2 Melt the butter in the microwave or a small saucepan.
3 Whisk together the eggs, vanilla and sugar in a mixing bowl over a saucepan of hand-hot water for 8–10 minutes or until the mixture is pale and thick, with the texture of softly whipped cream. Remove the bowl from the pan and continue whisking for a further 5 minutes.
4 Using a metal spoon, gently fold in the melted butter (leaving any sediment in the bottom of the bowl), the flour and the cocoa powder. Divide the mixture between the prepared tins.

5 Bake for 10–15 minutes. Remove from the oven and leave to cool in the tins for 5 minutes, then turn out onto a wire rack to cool completely.
6 Prick the cooled cakes all over with a skewer. Spoon the kirsch over the cakes and leave for 5 minutes.
7 Whip the cream until softly stiff. Sandwich the cakes together with about two-thirds of the whipped cream and pie filling. Spread the remaining cream over the top cake and spoon the remaining pie filling in the centre. Decorate the top with chocolate curls. Serve immediately.

TIP

To freeze, wrap the cooled cakes and freeze for up to 1 month. Defrost at room temperature and continue at Step 6.

Calories	Fibre	Salt	Sugar	Fat
588	1.4g	0.5g	36g	42g of which 25g is saturated

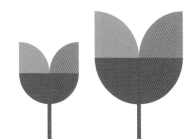

Lemon Meringue Pie

The combination of crisp pastry, a tangy lemon filling and a cloud of meringue meant that lemon meringue pie was a dessert the country couldn't get enough of when eggs finally came off ration in 1953. And there's still nothing to beat it!

SERVES 4-6   **PREPARATION** 25 minutes   **COOKING** 1 hour

Plain flour for dusting
Ready-rolled shortcrust pastry 320g pack
Cornflour 2 tbsp
Caster sugar 125g (4½oz)

Lemons 2 large, finely grated zest and juice
Eggs 2, separated
Butter 15g (½oz)

1 Preheat the oven to 200°C/180°fan/ Gas 6.

2 On a lightly floured surface, roll out the pastry a little more and use to line a 20cm (8in) loose-bottomed flan tin. Prick all over and line with baking paper and baking beans or dry rice. Bake the pastry case for 15 minutes.

3 Remove the paper and beans or rice and return the pastry case to the oven for a further 15 minutes or until crisp and golden. Remove from the oven and reduce the temperature to 150°C/ 130°fan/Gas 2.

4 To make the filling, put the cornflour, 50g (2oz) of the sugar and the lemon zest into a bowl. Add a little cold water and mix to a smooth paste. Heat 150ml (¼ pint) water with the lemon juice.

Combine with the paste then return to the saucepan and cook, stirring, until the mixture comes to the boil and thickens. Lower the heat and simmer for 3 minutes.

5 Beat in the egg yolks and butter and cook gently for a further minute then pour into the pastry case.

6 Put the egg whites into a grease-free bowl and whisk until stiff. Gently fold in the remaining sugar. Pile the meringue on top of the pie and bake for 20–30 minutes until pale golden.

7 Serve warm or leave to cool before slicing.

Calories	Fibre	Salt	Sugar	Fat
407	2g	0.4g	21g	21g of which 8g is saturated

Coconut Jam Sponge Pudding

An old school pudding, but made with butter and good jam it's so much better than the one you may remember from your schooldays.

SERVES 6 **PREPARATION** 15 minutes **COOKING** 15–20 minutes

Self-raising flour 110g (4oz)
Salt pinch
Butter 110g (4oz), softened
Caster sugar 110g (4oz)
Eggs 2, beaten

Milk 2 tbsp
Desiccated coconut 75g (3oz)
Strawberry jam 150g (5oz)
Custard to serve (optional)

1 Preheat the oven to 200°C/180°fan/ Gas 6. Butter a 1.5 litre (2½ pint) baking dish.
2 Sift the flour and salt into a bowl.
3 In a mixing bowl, cream the butter and sugar together until light and fluffy. Beat in the eggs, a little at a time, adding a spoonful of flour with each addition. Fold in the remaining flour with the milk and 50g (2oz) of the coconut. Spoon into the baking dish and bake for 15–20 minutes until just firm to the touch.
4 While still warm, spread with the jam and sprinkle with the remaining coconut.
5 Serve warm with custard, if you like, or cold.

TIPS

If you don't have any strawberry jam, try raspberry, cherry or pineapple jam, or chocolate hazelnut spread: first soften the spread in the microwave.
To microwave, cook the sponge on High for 3–4 minutes until risen and just firm to the touch. Leave to stand for 1 minute then spread with the jam.

Calories	Fibre	Salt	Sugar	Fat
443	3g	0.8g	36g	25g of which 17g is saturated

Eve's Pudding

Eve's pudding, also known as Mother Eve's pudding, has a light sponge topping with soft, sweetened apples underneath. It first appeared in the early nineteenth century and has remained a popular dessert ever since.

SERVES 4-5   **PREPARATION** 20 minutes   **COOKING** 1-1¼ hours

Cooking apples 450g (1lb), peeled, cored and sliced
Butter 110g (4oz), plus extra for greasing
Caster sugar 185g (6½oz)
Eggs 2, beaten

Self-raising flour 110g (4oz)
Salt pinch
Milk 2 tbsp
Custard or cream to serve (optional)

1 Preheat the oven to 180°C/160°fan/Gas 4. Arrange the apples in layers in a greased 1.5 litre (2½ pint) baking dish, sprinkling 75g (3oz) of the sugar between the layers.
2 Cream the butter and the remaining sugar together until light and fluffy. Beat in the eggs, a little at a time, adding a spoonful of flour with each addition. Fold in the remaining flour and the salt, alternating with tablespoons of milk.
3 Spoon the mixture over the apples. Bake for 1-1¼ hours or until a skewer inserted into the centre of the sponge comes out clean.
4 Serve hot, with custard or cream if you like.

TIP

Instead of apples, use gooseberries, rhubarb, plums, damsons, or apples mixed with blackberries.

Calories	Fibre	Salt	Sugar	Fat
472	2.5g	0.9g	46g	23g of which 13g is saturated

Pineapple Upside Down Pudding

In the 1920s an American producer of canned pineapple ran a recipe contest: an upside-down cake was among the winning recipes. Canned pineapple was unavailable in Britain in the 1940s and early 50s, but it made a successful comeback in this dessert in the 1960s.

SERVES 6   **PREPARATION** 10 minutes   **COOKING** 35 minutes

Butter 110g (4oz), softened, plus extra for greasing
Golden syrup 4 tbsp
Pineapple rings in juice 227g can, drained
Glacé cherries 5, halved

Caster sugar 110g (4oz)
Eggs 2, beaten
Self-raising flour 110g (4oz), sifted
Custard or cream to serve (optional)

1 Preheat the oven to 180°C/160°fan/ Gas 4. Grease and line a 20cm (8in) sandwich tin. Spoon in the golden syrup and arrange the pineapple rings on top, then place a glacé cherry half in each ring and arrange the remaining cherries around the tin.
2 Cream the butter and sugar together until light and fluffy.
3 Beat in the eggs one at a time, adding a spoonful of flour and beating well after each addition. Fold in the remaining flour.
4 Spoon the mixture evenly over the pineapple. Bake for about 35 minutes until just firm and golden. Leave the pudding in the tin for a few minutes, then turn out and serve hot or cold with custard or cream, if you like.

TIPS
Omit the golden syrup, if you prefer a less sweet pudding.
Add grated orange or lemon zest and juice to the sponge mixture.

VARIATION
Chocolate Upside Down Pudding Add 2 tablespoons of cocoa powder blended with 2 tablespoons of hot water to the sponge mixture. Use canned pear halves or pineapple rings.

Calories	Fibre	Salt	Sugar	Fat
389	1g	0.7g	35g	19g of which 11g is saturated

Syrup Sponge Pudding

First sold in 1883, golden syrup soon became an indispensable source of sticky sweetness in Britain's puddings. The stodgy school syrup suet pudding was actually loved by many children, but this light sponge version is just like mother (or grandma) used to make.

SERVES 4 **PREPARATION** 25 minutes **COOKING** 1½-2 hours

Butter 110g (4oz), softened, plus extra for greasing
Caster sugar 110g (4oz)
Eggs 2, beaten
Self-raising flour 110g (4oz), sifted

Salt pinch
Milk 2 tbsp
Golden syrup 3 tbsp
Single cream or custard to serve (optional)

1 Grease a 900ml (1½ pint) pudding basin and line the base with a disc of baking paper.
2 Cream the butter and sugar together until light and fluffy.
3 Beat in the eggs, a little at a time, adding a spoonful of flour and beating well after each addition.
4 Fold in the remaining flour and the salt, alternating with tablespoons of milk.
5 Spoon the syrup into the pudding basin then cover with the sponge mixture.
6 Cover the basin with baking paper, pleated to allow the pudding to rise, and secure with string.
7 Place on a metal trivet in a large saucepan. Add boiling water to come halfway up the sides of the basin. Cover the pan and steam for 1½-2 hours until well risen.
8 Turn out onto a serving plate and serve hot, with cream or custard.

TIP
To microwave, cover the basin with pleated baking paper as in Step 6 and cook on High for 5-7 minutes until well risen and firm to the touch. Leave to stand for 5 minutes before turning out.

VARIATIONS
■ **Chocolate Sponge Pudding** Use only 75g (3oz) flour and add 25g (1oz) cocoa powder. Omit the syrup.

■ **Fruit Sponge Pudding (sometimes referred to as Spotted Dick)** Stir in 50g (2oz) currants, sultanas or raisins after beating in the eggs. Omit the syrup.

■ **Jam Sponge Pudding** Replace the syrup with jam.

Calories	Fibre	Salt	Sugar	Fat
413	0g	1g	42g	26g of which 15g is saturated

Jam Roly Poly

Roly-poly pudding, or dog-in-a-basket(!) has been a favourite since Victorian times. Beatrix Potter wrote The Roly-Poly Pudding in 1908: it was later republished as The Tale of Samuel Whiskers.

SERVES 4   **PREPARATION** 20 minutes   **COOKING** 1½ hours

Self-raising flour 175g (6oz)
Salt pinch
Shredded vegetable suet 75g (3oz)

Jam 4–6 tbsp
Milk 1 tbsp
Custard to serve (optional)

1 Mix the flour, salt and suet together in a bowl.

2 Using a round-bladed knife, stir in 4–5 tablespoons of water to give a light, elastic dough. Knead very lightly until smooth.

3 Roll out to a rectangle about 23 x 25cm (9 x 10in) and spread with the jam. Brush the edges with milk and roll up, starting from the short end.

4 Make a 5cm (2in) pleat in a large piece of baking paper then wrap the pudding loosely to allow for expansion. Then wrap in foil, pleating the edges tightly together to seal. Tie the ends securely with string to form a cracker shape. Make a string handle across the top. Lower the roll into a large pan of boiling water, cover and boil for 1½ hours.

5 Lift the pudding out of the water using the string handle. Place on a wire rack standing over a tray and allow excess moisture to drain off.

6 Snip the string and gently roll the pudding onto a warmed serving plate. Slice and serve with custard if you like.

TIPS

Instead of boiling, roly-poly puddings can be baked, uncovered, at 200°C/180°fan/Gas 6 for about 40 minutes.
You can cook the paper-wrapped pudding in the microwave on High for 4–5 minutes. Leave to stand for 5 minutes before slicing.

VARIATIONS

◼ **Syrup Roly Poly** Instead of jam, spread the pastry with 60ml (4 tablespoons) golden syrup mixed with 2–3 tablespoons fresh white breadcrumbs.

◼ **Lemon Roly Poly** Add the finely grated zest of 1 lemon to the dough. Roll out and spread with 4–6 tablespoons lemon curd instead of jam.

◼ **Mincemeat Roly Poly** Add the finely grated zest of 1 orange to the dough. Roll out and spread with 4–6 tablespoons mincemeat instead of jam.

◼ **Spotted Dick or Dog** Replace half the flour with 110g (4oz) fresh breadcrumbs. Add 50g (2oz) caster sugar, 175g (6oz) currants, finely grated zest of 1 lemon and 75ml (5 tablespoons) milk. Mix and shape into a neat roll about 15cm (6in) long.

Calories	Fibre	Salt	Sugar	Fat
407	2g	0.6g	25g	17g of which 10g is saturated

Chocolate Pudding

Hats off to the cook who conjured this up. Under the chocolate sponge is a saucy layer which gives the pudding its alternative names: self-saucing pudding, chocolate puddle pudding, chocolate fudge pudding and chocolate magic pudding.

SERVES 4-6   **PREPARATION** 15 minutes   **COOKING** 15-20 minutes

Butter 75g (3oz), softened, plus extra for greasing
Soft light brown sugar 125g (4½oz)
Cocoa powder 5 tbsp
Self-raising flour 75g (3oz), sifted

Baking powder ½ tsp
Eggs 3
Boiling water 250ml (9fl oz)
Cream or vanilla ice cream to serve (optional)

1 Preheat the oven to 180°C/160°fan/Gas 4 and grease a 1.2 litre (2 pint) baking dish.
2 Beat together the butter, 75g (3oz) of the sugar, 3 tablespoons of the cocoa powder, the flour, baking powder and eggs. Spoon into the prepared dish and smooth the top.
3 Put the remaining sugar and cocoa powder in a heatproof bowl and gradually whisk in the boiling water. Pour over the pudding mixture.
4 Put the dish on a baking tray and bake for 15-20 minutes until the sponge is well risen (the sauce will have sunk to the bottom).
5 Serve immediately, with cream or ice cream if you like.

TIPS
In Step 2, add 3-4 pieces of finely chopped stem ginger, or the grated zest of 1 orange.
Add 2 teaspoons of peppermint extract with the boiling water.

Calories	Fibre	Salt	Sugar	Fat
295	2.5g	0.6g	20g	16g of which 9g is saturated

School Chocolate Cracknel
with Pink, Green or Chocolate Custard

Also known as chocolate concrete, this classic school pudding can be served with the famous (or infamous!) pink, green or chocolate custard.

SERVES 9   **PREPARATION** 15 minutes   **COOKING** 30–35 minutes

Plain flour 225g (8oz)
Cocoa powder 50g (2oz)
Caster sugar 175g (6oz)
Unsalted butter 175g (6oz), melted
Vanilla extract 1 tsp
Granulated sugar 2 tbsp

For the custard
Cornflour 15g (½oz)
Milk 300ml (½ pint)
Butter 15g (½oz)
Caster sugar 2 tbsp
Chocolate: Dark chocolate 25g (1oz), grated
Pink: Raspberry or vanilla extract ¼–½ tsp and a few drops of red food colouring
Green: Peppermint extract ¼–½ tsp and a few drops of green food colouring

1 Preheat the oven to 180°C/160C°fan/ Gas 4. Line a 20cm (8in) square tin with baking paper.
2 In a mixing bowl, mix together the flour, cocoa powder and caster sugar.
3 Stir in the melted butter and vanilla.
4 Spoon the mixture into the prepared tin and press down well with the back of a spoon.
5 Bake for 30–35 minutes until crusty at the edges. Sprinkle with the granulated sugar and leave to cool in the tin for 10 minutes.
6 Use the paper to lift the cracknel out of the tin. Cut into 9 squares and transfer to a wire rack to cool completely.

7 To make the custard: mix the cornflour to a smooth paste with a little of the milk. Heat the remaining milk in a saucepan until almost boiling, then pour onto the cornflour paste. Return the milk to the pan and simmer, whisking, for 2–3 minutes until smooth and thick.
8 Remove from the heat and whisk in the butter and sugar, plus the chocolate or extract and colouring, depending on your choice of custard.
9 Serve with the chocolate cracknel.

TIP
The cracknel can be eaten on its own but it is quite hard, hence the nickname concrete.

Calories	Fibre	Salt	Sugar	Fat
414	2g	0.6g	32g	21g of which 13g is saturated

Rice Pudding

Some of us remember the milk puddings of our childhood as the ultimate creamy comfort food, while to others they were the stuff of nightmares. Either way, it's worth giving them another go as they're so simple to make and can be cooked on a low shelf in the oven at the same time as your main course.

SERVES 6   **PREPARATION** 10 minutes   **COOKING** 2–2½ hours

Butter for greasing
Pudding rice 100g (3½oz)
Milk 1.25 litres (2 pints)

Caster sugar 50g (2oz)
Lemon zest 2 strips
Grated nutmeg

1 Preheat the oven to 150°C/130°fan/ Gas 2. Butter a 1.5 litre (2½ pint) baking dish.
2 Wash the rice and drain well. Put into the buttered dish and stir in the milk.
3 Add the sugar and lemon zest and stir well. Sprinkle with grated nutmeg.
4 Bake for 2–2½ hours, stirring after about 30 minutes.
5 Serve hot.

TIPS
Sweeten with honey instead of sugar.
Top with chopped tropical fruit.

VARIATIONS
■ **Tapioca Pudding** Replace the pudding rice with tapioca.

■ **Semolina Pudding** (Serves 4) Heat 600ml (1 pint) milk in a saucepan with 40g (1½oz) sugar, whisking constantly until almost boiling. Reduce the heat, whisk in 50g (2oz) semolina and continue whisking until thickened and smooth. Leave to stand for 5 minutes, then serve with a teaspoon of jam.

■ **Sago Pudding** Follow the method for semolina, using sago instead of semolina.

Calories	Fibre	Salt	Sugar	Fat
242	0.5g	0.3g	17g	10g of which 6g is saturated

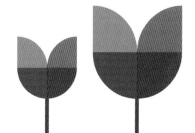

Baked Custards

Baked or 'egg' custards were often cooked in the oven alongside the roast for Sunday lunch. Thought to date back to medieval times, baked custards are silky, comforting desserts that take very little effort to make.

SERVES 2   **PREPARATION** 10 minutes plus chilling   **COOKING** 30 minutes   Ⓥ

Grated orange zest 1 tsp
Caster sugar 1 tbsp
Egg 1 medium, plus 1 **egg yolk**

Milk 200ml (7fl oz)
Ground cinnamon pinch

1 Preheat the oven to 180°C/160°fan/ Gas 4. Put the orange zest, sugar and egg plus egg yolk into a heatproof jug and whisk together.
2 Bring the milk just to the boil and gradually whisk it into the egg mixture. Pour into two ramekin dishes and sprinkle with cinnamon.
3 Put the dishes into a small roasting tin and pour in enough boiling water to come halfway up the sides of the dishes. Cook for 20–25 minutes or until the custards are set.
4 Leave to cool then chill before serving.

TIPS
You could put a few raisins, blueberries or cooked fruits into the ramekins before pouring in the custard mixture.
You could use lemon zest instead of orange, and top with nutmeg instead of cinnamon.

Calories	Fibre	Salt	Sugar	Fat
173	0.5g	0.2g	14g	9g of which 4g is saturated

Bread & Butter Pudding

Variations of this dish have been around for centuries: it's a simple way to use leftover bread, breadcrumbs or slightly stale cake, and the modern versions using brioche, panettone or hot cross buns are just the latest developments of this much-loved pudding.

SERVES 4   **PREPARATION** 10 minutes plus standing   **COOKING** 45 minutes–1 hour

White bread 6 thin slices, crusts removed
Butter 50g (2oz), plus extra for greasing
Sultanas 50g (2oz)
Caster sugar 40g (1½oz)

Eggs 2
Milk 600ml (1 pint)
Single cream, custard or vanilla ice cream to serve (optional)

1 Thickly spread the bread with butter. Cut into triangles. Put half into a 1.2 litre (2 pint) buttered baking dish. Sprinkle with all the sultanas and half of the sugar.
2 Top with the remaining bread, buttered side uppermost. Sprinkle with the remaining sugar.
3 Beat the eggs and milk together then pour over the bread. Leave to stand for 30 minutes, so that the bread absorbs some of the liquid.
4 Preheat the oven to 170°C/150°fan/Gas 3.
5 Bake for 45 minutes to 1 hour, until set and the top is crisp and golden.
6 Serve with cream, custard or ice cream, if you like.

VARIATION
■ **Osborne Pudding** Use brown bread and butter, spread with marmalade. Omit the dried fruit.

Calories	Fibre	Salt	Sugar	Fat
418	1.5g	1g	26g	21g of which 12g is saturated

Fruit Crumble

For most of us, crumble is a favourite pudding from our childhood, yet it first appeared in a Ministry of Food leaflet published during the Second World War. It's rarely seen without a partner: custard, cream or ice cream – or in some families, all three!

SERVES 4   **PREPARATION** 15 minutes   **COOKING** 50 minutes

Fruit such as cooking apples, rhubarb, gooseberries, plums, damsons, blackberries or blueberries 900g (2lb), washed or peeled and sliced, as appropriate
Caster sugar 75–110g (3–4oz), depending on the sharpness of the fruit

Plain flour 150g (5oz)
Butter 110g (4oz), cubed
Rolled oats 50g (2oz)
Brown sugar 110g (4oz)
Custard, cream or vanilla ice cream to serve

1 Preheat the oven to 180°C/160°fan/ Gas 4.
2 Put the fruit in a saucepan with the caster sugar. Cook gently for about 5 minutes or until softened. Spoon into a 1.2 litre (2 pint) baking dish.
3 Put the flour in a bowl then rub in the butter until the mixture resembles breadcrumbs. Stir in the oats and brown sugar.
4 Sprinkle the mixture evenly over the fruit. Put the dish on a baking tray and bake for about 45 minutes until the top is light brown.
5 Leave to cool for a few minutes before serving with custard, cream or ice cream.

TIPS
Use frozen fruit, defrosted and gently heated, or well drained canned fruit for a storecupboard dessert.
Add a pinch of ground cinnamon to apples or plums, or ground ginger to rhubarb, if you like.

Calories	Fibre	Salt	Sugar	Fat
663	8.5g	0.5g	69g	25g of which 15g is saturated

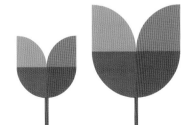

Butterscotch Apple Pie

'Good apple pies are a considerable part of our domestic happiness,' wrote Jane Austen in a letter to her sister in 1815. And in 1845 Eliza Acton's cookery book mentions an 'old-fashioned creamed apple tart' in which a rich custard is poured into the tart. Here's another twist on the apple pie, aimed at the sweet-toothed.

SERVES 6 **PREPARATION** 20 minutes **COOKING** 30–35 minutes

Light muscovado sugar 75g (3oz)
Golden syrup 1 tbsp
Butter 75g (3oz)
Cornflour 1 tbsp
Lemon juice 1 tbsp
Cooking apples 900g (2lb), peeled, cored and thickly sliced

Ready-rolled sweet pastry 320g pack
Milk to brush
Caster sugar 1 tbsp
Cream to serve (optional)

1 Preheat the oven to 200°C/180°fan/Gas 6.
2 Put the muscovado sugar, syrup and butter in a pan and heat gently until the butter has melted and the sugar has dissolved. Mix the cornflour with the lemon juice and add to the sauce. Heat, stirring, until thickened.
3 Put the apples in a pie dish and pour over the butterscotch sauce.
4 Place the pastry on a lightly floured surface and cut out a lid for the pie and a long strip of pastry about 1cm (½in) wide. Dampen the rim of the pie dish and put the strip of pastry around it. Dampen the pastry strip and cover with the pastry lid, pressing together with a fork to seal.
5 Cut out leaves or other shapes from the pastry trimmings to decorate the pie. Make a slit in the top, brush the pastry with milk and sprinkle with caster sugar.
6 Bake for 25–30 minutes until golden. Serve warm, with cream if you like.

TIP
Keep stirring the butterscotch sauce as you make it so that the sauce doesn't stick on the bottom of the pan.

Calories	Fibre	Salt	Sugar	Fat
520	4g	0.5g	41g	28g of which 13g is saturated

Treacle Tart

The word 'treacle' is misleading: this sweet tart has always been made with golden syrup, which became widely available in the 1880s.

SERVES 6-8 **PREPARATION** 10 minutes **COOKING** 30 minutes

Shortcrust pastry 250g (9oz)
Golden syrup 450g (1 lb)
Ground ginger 1 tsp
Fresh breadcrumbs (white or brown) 110g (4oz)

Icing sugar for sifting
Pouring cream to serve (optional)

1 Preheat the oven to 200°C/180°fan/ Gas 6.
2 Roll out the pastry and use to line a 20cm (8in) fluted flan tin.
3 Warm the golden syrup in a saucepan. Stir in the ginger and the breadcrumbs then pour the mixture into the pastry case. Bake for 20–25 minutes until just set.
4 Sift a little icing sugar over the tart and serve warm or cold, with cream, if you like.

TIP
Use the grated zest of 1 lemon and 2 teaspoons of lemon juice instead of the ginger, if you prefer.
For speed, use a ready-rolled shortcrust pastry sheet, rolled out a little larger. Use any trimmings to make jam tarts.

Calories	Fibre	Salt	Sugar	Fat
274	1.5g	0.5g	27g	10g of which 4g is saturated

Bakes & Treats

142   BAKEWELL TART

145   MANCHESTER TART

146   FRUIT SLICE (FLY PIE)

149   CHOC MINT BARS

150   CHERRY COCONUT CHOC TRAYBAKE

153   SHREWSBURY BISCUITS

154   ROCK CAKES

157   TOTTENHAM CAKE

158   PINEAPPLE & COCONUT FRUIT LOAF

161   HEDGEHOG CELEBRATION CAKE
      (ALSO SWEETSHOP CELEBRATION CAKE)

162   BOILED FRUIT CHRISTMAS CAKE

165   KRISPIE CAKES

166   TIFFIN

169   PEPPERMINT CREAMS
      (ALSO CHOCOLATE PEPPERMINT CREAMS)

169   WHITE CHOCOLATE FUDGE
      (ALSO CHOCOLATE BAR FUDGE,
      MILK CHOCOLATE FUDGE)

170   COCONUT ICE

170   BUTTERSCOTCH

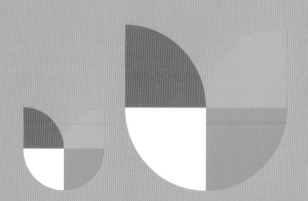

Bakewell Tart

Originally from Bakewell in Derbyshire, an early published recipe used no pastry, but puff pastry is considered to be authentic (sometimes known as Bakewell Pudding). Today's commercial Bakewell tarts are quite different, with a sweet pastry base and white icing on top.

SERVES 6   **PREPARATION** 30 minutes   **COOKING** 30–35 minutes

Butter 50g (2oz), softened, plus extra for greasing
Flour for dusting
Puff pastry 250g (9oz)
Raspberry jam 75g (3oz)
Ground almonds 110g (4oz)

Caster sugar 110g (4oz)
Eggs 3, beaten
Almond essence ¼ tsp
Icing sugar for sifting
Custard or cream to serve

1 Preheat the oven to 200°C/180°fan/ Gas 6 and put a baking sheet in the oven. Butter a 900ml (1½ pint) shallow pie dish.

2 On a lightly floured surface, roll out the pastry and use to line the pie dish. Trim off any excess pastry. Knock up the pastry edge with a knife to help the pastry layers rise well.

3 Spread the jam over the base of the pastry case and chill while you make the filling.

4 In a large bowl, beat together the almonds, sugar, softened butter, eggs and almond essence. Spoon the mixture over the jam and smooth the top.

5 Place the pie dish on the hot baking sheet and bake for 30–35 minutes until the filling has set.

6 Sift a little icing sugar over the tart and serve hot with custard or cold with cream.

TIPS
You could sprinkle a handful of flaked almonds over the filling before baking. If you like, mix 75g (3oz) icing sugar with a teaspoon of warm water to make a thick, smooth icing; drizzle over the tart in random zigzag patterns.

Calories	Fibre	Salt	Sugar	Fat
494	1g	0.7g	28g	32g of which 12g is saturated

Manchester Tart

A staple on school dinner menus until the mid-1980s. Manchester Tart is a variation on an earlier Manchester Pudding recipe by the Victorian cookery writer Mrs Beeton. This simple version uses the retro classic: custard powder. Developed because his wife was allergic to eggs, Bird's Custard was formulated by Alfred Bird in 1837 at his chemist's shop in Birmingham.

SERVES 6–8   **PREPARATION** 30 minutes plus chilling   **COOKING** 25 minutes

For the pastry
Plain flour 175g (6oz), plus extra for dusting
Salt pinch
Butter 75g (3oz), chilled and cubed
Icing sugar 1 tbsp
Egg yolks 2

For the filling
Custard powder 2 heaped tbsp
Caster sugar 2 tbsp
Milk 600ml (1 pint)
Seedless raspberry jam 75g (3oz)
Desiccated coconut 25g (1oz)
Glacé cherry 1 (optional)

1 Put the flour, salt, butter, icing sugar and egg yolks into a food processor then whizz together. Briefly knead on a lightly floured surface to bring the pastry together. Wrap and chill for 15 minutes.
2 On a floured surface (or between two sheets of baking paper), roll out the pastry and use to line a 20cm (8in) loose-bottomed flan tin (see Tip). Prick the base with a fork and chill for 15 minutes. Preheat the oven to 220°C/200°fan/Gas 7.
3 Make the custard: put the custard powder and caster sugar in a non-stick saucepan and add a little of the milk. Mix to a paste and then add the remaining milk, stirring. Bring to the boil, stirring continuously, and then pour into a jug.
4 Line the pastry case with baking paper and baking beans or dry rice, then bake for 10 minutes. Remove the paper and

beans or rice, reduce the temperature to 190°C/170°fan/Gas 5 and bake for a further 10 minutes or until the pastry is crisp. Leave to cool.
5 Spoon the jam into the pastry case and spread over the base. Cover with half of the coconut. Top with the custard (you may need to remove the skin) then the remaining coconut. Finish with a cherry in the centre, if using.
6 Chill for 1 hour before slicing.

TIPS

If you find the pastry difficult to roll out, place the ball of dough in the centre of the tin and use a large metal spoon to press it out to the edges and then up the sides of the tin. Or, for convenience, buy a ready-made sweet pastry case.

Calories	Fibre	Salt	Sugar	Fat
309	1.5g	0.4g	17g	14g of which 9g is saturated

Fruit Slice

Affectionately(!) known as fly pie or fly cemetery, this has a crisp pastry base and top and is packed full of gently spiced sticky currants. A similar bake – sometimes called Nelson squares – has a filling that includes leftover cake.

MAKES 10 slices   **PREPARATION** 20 minutes plus chilling   **COOKING** 45 minutes

For the pastry
Plain flour 350g (12oz), plus extra for dusting
Salt ¼ tsp
Butter 225g (8oz), chilled and cubed
Milk to brush
Granulated sugar 2 tbsp

For the filling
Butter 50g (2oz), cubed
Light muscovado sugar 110g (4oz)
Mixed spice 1½ tsp
Apricot jam 2 tbsp
Currants 375g (13oz)

1 To make the pastry, put the flour, salt and butter into a food processor and whizz to make a dough. Wrap and chill for at least 30 minutes.

2 To make the filling, gently heat the butter, muscovado sugar, spice, jam and currants until the butter has melted and everything is combined.

3 Preheat the oven to 180°C/160°fan/Gas 4.

4 Cut the pastry in half. Place one half on a piece of baking paper and roll out using a floured rolling pin to a rectangle about 30 x 20cm (12 x 8in).

5 Lift the baking paper and pastry onto a baking tray and spread with the currant mixture almost to the edges. Roll out the remaining pastry on another piece of baking paper to the same size. Turn the paper over so that the pastry covers the currant mixture and carefully peel the paper away. Press the edges together and trim to neaten, if necessary. Prick the top evenly with a fork and brush with a little milk.

6 Bake for 30 minutes, then sprinkle with granulated sugar. Return to the oven for a further 10 minutes or until the pastry is golden and crisp. Leave to cool on the tray.

7 When completely cold, cut into 10 pieces and store in an airtight container.

TIPS

If the pastry doesn't stick together add 1–2 teaspoons of cold water to the food processor and whizz again.

If you find the baking paper is slipping when rolling out the pastry, fold it over the edge of the work surface and lean on the paper while rolling.

This bake is much easier to cut when cold, but you could carefully slice a piece or two and serve warm with cream if you like – be careful as the filling is very hot!

Calories	Fibre	Salt	Sugar	Fat
504	3g	0.8g	43g	23g of which 14g is saturated

Choc Mint Bars

Were these inspired by After Eight mints, created in
1962 and still going strong? You can serve these mint
bars after dinner or pass them round while watching TV.

MAKES 10 bars   **PREPARATION** 20 minutes plus cooling   **COOKING** 15 minutes

Butter 110g (4oz), softened, plus extra for
greasing
Caster sugar 110g (4oz)
Plain flour 175g (6oz)

Icing sugar 175g (6oz)
Peppermint extract ½ tsp
Dark chocolate 175g (6oz), chopped

1 Preheat the oven to 180°C/160°fan/
Gas 4 and grease a 25 x 18cm (10 x 7in)
baking tin.
2 Cream the butter and caster sugar
together until pale and fluffy. Mix in
the flour and knead to make a smooth
dough. Press into the tin, prick all over
with a fork, then bake for 15 minutes.
Leave to cool in the tin.
3 In a bowl, mix the icing sugar with 1–2
tablespoons of water and the peppermint
extract, then spread over the shortbread
base. Leave to set.
4 Melt the chocolate in a heatproof bowl
over a pan of barely simmering water.
Spread over the icing and leave in the tin
to cool.
5 When set, cut into bars. Store in an
airtight container.

TIP
For chocolate shortbread, use only 150g
(5oz) flour and add 25g (1oz) cocoa
powder.

Calories	Fibre	Salt	Sugar	Fat
349	1.3g	0.2g	39g	15g of which 9g is saturated

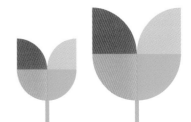

Cherry Coconut Choc Traybake

Glacé cherries were introduced to Britain from France in the late 1800s and have been used often in baking ever since. Many traybake recipes like this would have been written by hand and passed down through generations.

MAKES 16 squares   **PREPARATION** 15 minutes plus cooling   **COOKING** 30 minutes

Dark or milk chocolate 300g (11oz), chopped
Glacé cherries 200g (7oz), halved

Eggs 4
Caster sugar 175g (6oz)
Desiccated coconut 250g (9oz)

1 Preheat the oven to 180°C/160°fan/ Gas 4 and line a 23cm (9in) square tin with baking paper, leaving a slight overhang.

2 Melt the chocolate in a heatproof bowl over a pan of barely simmering water. Stir from time to time until the chocolate has melted.

3 Spread the melted chocolate across the base of the tin and scatter with the cherries.

4 In a mixing bowl, beat together the eggs and sugar, then fold in the coconut. Spoon over the cherries.

5 Bake for 20–25 minutes until golden and just set. Leave to cool completely in the tin.

6 Cut into 16 squares. Store in an airtight container in the fridge.

TIP
Use raisins or dried tropical fruit instead of glacé cherries, if you prefer.

Calories	Fibre	Salt	Sugar	Fat
289	3.5g	0.1g	23g	16g of which 12g is saturated

Shrewsbury Biscuits

The Shropshire town was known for its crisp flat 'cakes' as long ago as the sixteenth century; one of the most famous producers was a Mr Pailin, said to have begun making them in 1760. These biscuits were bought as gifts by visitors to Shrewsbury in much the same way as shortbread in Scotland or clotted cream in Devon. They have a light texture and lemony flavour and are very simple to prepare.

MAKES 24   **PREPARATION** 15 minutes   **COOKING** 12–15 minutes

Butter 110g (4oz), plus extra for greasing
Caster sugar 150g (5oz), plus extra for sprinkling
Egg yolks 2

Plain flour 225g (8oz)
Lemon 1, finely grated zest
Dried mixed fruit 50g (2oz)

1 Preheat the oven to 180°C/160°fan/Gas 4 and butter two non-stick baking sheets.
2 Cream the butter and sugar together until pale and fluffy. Add the egg yolks and beat well. Add the flour, lemon zest and fruit and mix to a fairly firm dough.
3 On a lightly floured surface, knead lightly and then roll out to about 5mm (¼in) thick. Cut out 6.5cm (2½in) rounds with a fluted cutter and place on the baking sheets. Sprinkle with a little extra caster sugar.
4 Bake for 12–15 minutes until lightly browned and firm to the touch. Cool on wire racks. Store in an airtight container.

TIP

If you like spiced biscuits, omit the lemon zest and add 1 teaspoon mixed spice and 1 teaspoon ground cinnamon instead.

Calories	Fibre	Salt	Sugar	Fat
106	0.4g	0.1g	8g	4.5g of which 3g is saturated

Rock Cakes

If you're of a certain age, you may remember proudly taking rock cakes home from your first cookery lesson. Get the children to help make these little cakes, or rustle them up yourself as an easy treat for afternoon tea.

MAKES 12   **PREPARATION** 15 minutes   **COOKING** 15 minutes

Butter 75g (3oz), cubed, plus extra for greasing
Self-raising flour 225g (8oz)
Dried mixed fruit 75g (3oz)

Caster sugar 75g (3oz), plus extra for sprinkling
Egg 1, beaten
Salt pinch

1 Preheat the oven to 190°C/170°fan/ Gas 5 and grease a baking sheet.
2 Sift the flour into a bowl then rub in the butter until the mixture resembles breadcrumbs.
3 Stir in the fruit, sugar, egg and salt. Use a fork to work the mixture together to form a stiff dough.
4 Divide the mixture into 12 roughly shaped balls and place them on the prepared baking sheet. Sprinkle a little extra caster sugar over the cakes.
5 Bake for 12–15 minutes until light golden.
6 Cool on a wire rack. Store in an airtight container for up to 3 days.

TIPS
Add a pinch of mixed spice if you like. Any dried fruits may be used: for example, dried apricots with a little ground cinnamon work well.

Calories	Fibre	Salt	Sugar	Fat
165	1g	0.4g	12g	6g of which 3.5g is saturated

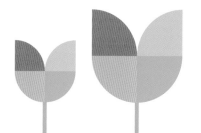

Tottenham Cake

Thomas Chalkley, a baker in the North London suburb of Tottenham in the nineteenth century, was a Quaker who wanted to create a large cake suitable for sharing. He coloured the icing with mulberry juice from the mulberry tree in the garden of the Friends (Quakers) Meeting House.

MAKES 16 squares   **PREPARATION** 15 minutes   **COOKING** 25–30 minutes   Ⓥ

Butter 175g (6oz), softened
Self-raising flour 175g (6oz), sifted
Baking powder ½ tsp
Caster sugar 175g (6oz)
Eggs 3

Vanilla extract 1 tsp
Icing sugar 300g (11oz), sifted
Red food colouring a few drops
Colourful sprinkles to decorate

1 Preheat the oven to 180°C/160°fan/ Gas 4 and line a 25 x 20cm (10 x 8in) baking tin with baking paper.
2 Put the butter, flour, baking powder, sugar, eggs and vanilla in a food processor and whizz until combined (or mix in a bowl with an electric whisk).
3 Pour the mixture into the prepared tin and bake for 25–30 minutes until well risen, and a skewer inserted into the centre comes out clean.

4 Cool in the tin for 10 minutes, then turn out and cool completely on a wire rack.
5 Beat the icing sugar with 3 tablespoons of water and the food colouring. Spread the icing all over the sponge and scatter with sprinkles. Leave to set.
6 Slice into 16 squares and serve or store in an airtight container.

Calories	Fibre	Salt	Sugar	Fat
252	0.4g	0.4g	30g	10g of which 6g is saturated

Pineapple & Coconut Fruit Loaf

Pineapple, whether fresh or canned, was a treat in the early twentieth century, but was not available during the Second World War and the rationing that continued into the 1950s. By the 1960s cooks were becoming more confident in using exotic ingredients; they found that pineapple made a really moist loaf cake.

SERVES 10   **PREPARATION** 15 minutes   **COOKING** 40–45 minutes

Butter 110g (4oz), softened, plus extra for greasing
Self-raising flour 150g (5oz)
Caster sugar 75g (3oz)
Desiccated coconut 75g (3oz)

Eggs 2
Pineapple chunks in juice 227g can, drained (reserve the juice) and chopped
Luxury dried mixed fruit 75g (3oz)
Granulated sugar 2 tbsp

1 Preheat the oven to 190°C/170°fan/ Gas 5. Grease and line a 900g (2lb) loaf tin with baking paper, leaving a slight overhang.
2 In a mixing bowl, mix together the flour, caster sugar, 50g (2oz) of the coconut, the butter and eggs. Fold in the pineapple chunks and dried fruit. Spoon into the prepared tin and smooth the top. Sprinkle with the remaining coconut.

3 Bake for 40–45 minutes until a skewer inserted into the centre comes out clean (cover with foil if the top is browning too quickly).
4 Mix 5 tablespoons of the reserved pineapple juice with the granulated sugar. As soon as the cake is cooked, spoon the juice over the cake.
5 Leave to cool in the tin for 10 minutes, then lift out of the tin and cool on a wire rack. Store in an airtight container.

Calories	Fibre	Salt	Sugar	Fat
274	2.3g	0.4g	19g	15g of which 10g is saturated

Hedgehog Celebration Cake

With rationing over and electric mixers becoming more widely available, the late 1950s saw a revival of home baking, including imaginative designs for children's party cakes. This hedgehog cake with chocolate button 'spines' was a familiar character at parties during the 1970s and 80s.

SERVES 12   **PREPARATION** 45 minutes   **COOKING** 20–25 minutes

For the cake
Butter 175g (6oz), softened, plus extra for greasing
Self-raising flour 175g (6oz), sifted
Caster sugar 175g (6oz)
Eggs 3
Vanilla extract 1 tsp
Cocoa powder 1 heaped tbsp, sifted

For the buttercream
Butter 225g (8oz), softened
Icing sugar 300g (11oz), sifted
Cocoa powder 2 tbsp, sifted
Vanilla extract 1 tsp
Milk 1–2 tbsp

To decorate
Chocolate buttons, glacé cherry, candy eyes

1 Preheat the oven to 180°C/160°fan/Gas 4. Grease two deep 18cm (7in) sandwich tins and line the bases with baking paper.
2 Put all the cake ingredients in a food processor and whizz until combined (or mix in a bowl with an electric whisk).
3 Divide the mixture between the tins and bake for 20–25 minutes or until risen and firm to touch.
4 Turn out and cool on a wire rack. When cold, cut 4.5cm (2in) from each side of each cake, giving you six pieces of cake.
5 For the buttercream, beat the butter, icing sugar and cocoa together with the vanilla extract until thick but spreadable: add a little milk to loosen if needed.
6 Place one of the centre cake pieces on a board or plate and spread the top with buttercream. Place the other centre piece on top and spread with more buttercream. On top of this, add the remaining four pieces, cut side down (curve up), sandwiching them together with buttercream. This will give you a curved back for the hedgehog.
7 Cut the edges off the front to make a pointed nose.
8 Spread the remaining buttercream all over the hedgehog, add a glacé cherry for the nose, add the eyes, then cover the body with chocolate buttons.

TIPS
As the cakes need to hold together vertically, you may need to bake for slightly longer than you usually would to ensure they're firm (but not dry).

VARIATION
■ **Sweetshop Celebration Cake** Leave the cakes intact, sandwich together and cover with buttercream. Top with sweets in concentric circles, or at random.

Calories	Fibre	Salt	Sugar	Fat
524	1.5g	0.8g	43g	32g of which 20g is saturated

Boiled Fruit Christmas Cake

This easy Christmas cake is based on the Dairy Diary boiled fruit cake, which has been a favourite for generations. You can enjoy it un-iced for a special afternoon tea, or finish with the simple, elegant Christmas decoration suggested here.

MAKES 12 slices   **PREPARATION** 45 minutes   **COOKING** 1½ hours

Dried mixed fruit 350g (12oz)
Glacé cherries 150g (5oz), chopped
Mixed peel 50g (2oz)
Walnuts 50g (2oz), chopped
Soft brown sugar 175g (6oz)
Butter 110g (4oz)
Mixed spice 1 tsp
Bicarbonate of soda ½ tsp
Milk 300ml (½ pint)
Self-raising flour 350g (12oz), sifted

Eggs 2, beaten

To decorate

Apricot jam 4 tbsp, warmed
Ready-rolled marzipan 400g pack
Icing sugar for dusting
Ready-to-roll fondant icing 1kg pack
Egg white 1, beaten
Edible white glitter

1 Preheat the oven to 160°C/140°fan/Gas 3. Line a deep 20cm (8in) cake tin with baking paper.
2 Place all the ingredients except the flour and eggs into a saucepan, bring to the boil and simmer for 5 minutes. Cool slightly.
3 Add the flour and eggs and stir well. Tip the cake mixture into the prepared tin and level the surface.
4 Bake for 40 minutes, then reduce the temperature to 150°C/130°fan/Gas 2 and cook for a further 40–45 minutes or until a skewer comes out clean.
5 Leave to cool in the tin for 5 minutes, then turn out onto a wire rack. Remove the paper and leave until cold.
6 To decorate, place the cake on a plate and brush with some of the jam. Unroll the marzipan and lift over the cake. Gently smooth over the top and sides of the cake and trim any excess with a sharp knife.

7 Brush the remaining jam over the marzipan. On a surface sprinkled with icing sugar, knead 850g (1lb 14oz) of the fondant icing until pliable, then roll out until it is large enough to cover the top and sides of the cake. Lift the icing onto the cake, smooth it down and around the sides, and trim excess from the bottom with a sharp knife. Smooth the icing with your palms, rubbing to buff it to a shine.
8 Roll out the remaining icing and cut out stars or snowflakes. Brush each with a little egg white then stick to the cake. Brush with more egg white and sprinkle with edible glitter. Leave to set.
9 Store in an airtight tin for up to 1 month.

TIP

If you prefer an un-iced cake, brush with apricot jam and gently push candied fruit or nuts onto the cake.

Calories	Fibre	Salt	Sugar	Fat
859	3.5g	0.8g	137g	17g of which 6g is saturated

Krispie Cakes

Rice Krispies were created in 1927, followed by the Mars Bar in 1932. Home economist Mildred Day was tasked by Kellogg's to create recipes for the back of Rice Krispies cereal packets. This 1970s treat was probably influenced by one of Mildred's recipes.

MAKES 16 squares   **PREPARATION** 15 minutes plus chilling   **COOKING** 5 minutes

Mars bars 3, chopped
Butter 50g (2oz), cubed

Rice Krispies 75g (3oz)
Dark chocolate 175g (6oz), chopped

1 Line the base and sides of a 23cm (9in) square baking tin with baking paper, leaving a slight overhang.
2 Melt the Mars bars and butter in a saucepan over a low heat.
3 Remove from the heat and stir in the Rice Krispies. Spoon into the prepared tin and chill for 1 hour until firm.
4 Melt the chocolate in a heatproof bowl over a pan of barely simmering water, stirring from time to time until the chocolate has melted.
5 Spread the chocolate over the Rice Krispies. Cool and then chill for a further hour until set.
6 Use the paper to lift the cake out of the tin. Cut into 16 squares. Store in an airtight container.

TIPS
Use cornflakes instead of Rice Krispies, and milk chocolate instead of dark, if preferred.
Make individual cakes in fairy cake cases, without the chocolate topping.

Calories	Fibre	Salt	Sugar	Fat
146	0.6g	0.1g	14g	7.5g of which 4g is saturated

Tiffin

A no-bake treat, also known as chocolate fridge cake or chocolate biscuit cake. Tiffin, an Anglo-Indian word for a light meal, was used for the bars of milk chocolate with biscuits and fruit introduced by Fry's chocolate company in 1937.

MAKES 16 squares   **PREPARATION** 20 minutes plus chilling
COOKING 5 minutes   Ⓥ Ⓕ

Dark chocolate 150g (5oz), broken into pieces
Butter 50g (2oz)

Golden syrup 3 tbsp
Nice biscuits 200g (7oz)
Sultanas 75g (3oz)

1 Line the base and sides of an 18cm (7in) square shallow tin with baking paper, leaving a slight overhang.
2 Put the chocolate into a saucepan with the butter and syrup. Heat gently, stirring occasionally, until it has melted. Remove from the heat.
3 Put the biscuits into a bag and crush them into small pieces with a rolling pin.
4 Stir the biscuits and sultanas into the chocolate mixture until they are evenly coated. Spoon into the prepared tin, level the surface and chill for 2–3 hours until set.
5 Use the paper to lift the tiffin out of the tin. Cut into 16 squares. Store in an airtight container.

TIPS
Add 1 tablespoon of chopped glacé ginger with the sultanas. Replace the Nice biscuits with digestives (or any biscuit you fancy). Top with an extra layer of melted milk or dark chocolate for an extra indulgent treat.
Wrap individual squares and freeze for up to 1 month. Defrost at room temperature on a wire rack for about an hour or until thoroughly defrosted.

Calories	Fibre	Salt	Sugar	Fat
153	0.8g	0.2g	15g	7g of which 4g is saturated

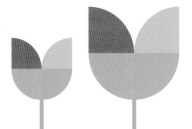

Peppermint Creams

MAKES 20–30
PREPARATION
15 minutes plus setting

Icing sugar 450g (1lb),
sifted, plus extra for
dusting
Cream of tartar ½ tsp
Evaporated milk 4–5 tbsp
Peppermint extract a few
drops

1 In a mixing bowl, mix
together the icing sugar,
cream of tartar and
evaporated milk to make
a pliable icing.
2 Add peppermint extract
to taste and then knead
on a surface dusted with
icing sugar.
3 Roll out to 3mm (⅛in)
thick. Cut into rounds or
other shapes with a small
biscuit cutter.

4 Carefully transfer to
a tray and leave for 24
hours until firm. Store in
an airtight container.

VARIATION
■ **Chocolate Peppermint
Creams** Half dip the
rounds in melted plain
chocolate – or drizzle
melted chocolate over the
top – and leave to set on
a sheet of baking paper.

White Chocolate Fudge

MAKES 36 pieces
PREPARATION
5 minutes plus chilling
COOKING 5 mins V

White chocolate 500g
(1lb 2oz), chopped
**Sweetened condensed
milk** 397g can

1 Line a 20cm (8in) square
shallow tin with two strips
of baking paper, leaving a
slight overhang.
2 In a pan, gently melt
together the chocolate
and condensed milk,
stirring occasionally, until
thick and smooth.
3 Pour into the prepared
tin, smooth the top and
chill for 4 hours.
4 Remove from the tin and
cut into 36 squares. Store
in an airtight container for
up to 2 weeks.

VARIATIONS
■ **Chocolate Bar Fudge**
When the pan is off the
heat, add chunks of your
favourite chocolate bar, or
chocolatey sweets, such
as Maltesers, Smarties or
Mini Eggs.

■ **Milk Chocolate Fudge**
Replace the white
chocolate with milk
chocolate.

Coconut Ice

MAKES 50 pieces
PREPARATION 10 minutes plus setting
COOKING 15 minutes (V)

Milk 75ml (2½fl oz)
Granulated sugar 450g (1lb)
Butter 15g (½oz)
Desiccated coconut 110g (4oz)
Vanilla extract ½ tsp
Pink food colouring a few drops

1 Line an 18cm (7in) square tin with baking paper
2 Pour the milk and 75ml (2½fl oz) water into a saucepan and bring to the boil.
3 Add the sugar and butter and heat gently, stirring until the sugar dissolves. Bring to the boil, cover the pan and boil gently for 2 minutes.
4 Uncover and continue to boil steadily, stirring occasionally, for 7–10 minutes or until a little of the mixture, dropped into a cup of cold water, forms a soft ball when rolled gently between finger and thumb. The temperature on a sugar thermometer, if using, should be 116°C (240°F). Remove from the heat.
5 Add the coconut and vanilla, then beat briskly until the mixture is thick and creamy.
6 Pour half into the prepared tin. Quickly colour the remainder pale pink and spread over the white layer.
7 Leave in the tin until firm and set, then cut into squares. Store in an airtight container.

Butterscotch

MAKES 18 pieces
PREPARATION 5 minutes plus setting
COOKING 25 minutes (V)

Butter 50g (2oz), plus extra for greasing
Demerara sugar 450g (1lb)

1 Grease a 15cm (6in) square tin.
2 Pour 150ml (¼ pint) water into a saucepan and bring to the boil. Add the sugar and butter and heat gently, stirring until the sugar dissolves. Bring to the boil, cover the pan and boil gently for 2 minutes.
3 Uncover and continue to boil, without stirring, for 8–12 minutes or until a little of the mixture, dropped into a cup of cold water, separates into hard brittle threads. The temperature on a sugar thermometer, if using, should be about 138°C (280°F).
4 Pour into the greased tin. When almost set, mark into squares or bars with a buttered knife.
5 When hard, break along the marked lines. Store in an airtight container.

Index

almonds
  Bakewell tart 142
  coronation chicken sandwiches 20
apples, *as alternative ingredient* 104
  butterscotch apple pie 136
  chicken curry 49
  Eve's pudding 116
  fruit crumble 135
apricots, *as alternative ingredient* 95, 154
Arctic roll 96
aubergines, vegetarian moussaka 37
autumn pudding 104

bacon, *as alternative ingredient* 33, 58
  coq au vin 53
  ham with pease pudding 61
  leek & bacon stovies 54
  liver & bacon with onion gravy 69
  quiche Lorraine 57
baked custards 131
Bakewell tart 142
beef, *as alternative ingredient* 58
  beef Stroganoff 86
  bubble & squeak 30
  corned beef hash 77
  farmhouse mince 78
  lobby 85
  mince & onion pie 81
  potted beef 24
  steak & kidney pudding 89
  steak Diane 90
  Teviotdale pie 82
biscuits
  Shrewsbury biscuits 153
  tiffin 166
Black Forest gateau 111
blackberries, *as alternative ingredient* 104, 116
  fruit crumble 135
blancmange 99
blueberries, *as alternative ingredient* 131
  fruit crumble 135
bread, *as alternative ingredient* 12, 86
  bread & butter pudding 132
  coronation chicken sandwiches 20
  French onion soup with cheese toasts 15
  melba toast 24
  veggie burgers 38
  Welsh rarebit 23
broccoli, *as alternative ingredient* 49
  broccoli & Stilton quiche 57
  buck rarebit 23
Brussels sprouts, *as alternative ingredient* 30
bubble & squeak 30
buck rarebit 23

burgers, veggie 38
butternut squash, *as alternative ingredient* 49, 74
butterscotch 170
butterscotch apple pie 136
butterscotch delight 100

cabbage
  bubble & squeak 30
  corned beef hash 77
cakes and bakes
  Black Forest gateau 111
  boiled fruit Christmas cake 162
  cherry coconut choc traybake 150
  choc mint bars 149
  hedgehog celebration cake 161
  krispie cakes 165
  rock cakes 154
  tiffin 166
  Tottenham cake 157
carrots, *as alternative ingredient* 30
  leek & bacon stovies 54
  lobby 85
  mince & onion pie 81
  shepherd's pie 74
  Teviotdale pie 82
cauliflower cheese 29
cheese
  broccoli & Stilton quiche 57
  buck rarebit 23
  cauliflower cheese 29
  cheese straws 11
  crispy pancakes 58
  French onion soup with cheese toasts 15
  leek & cheese quiche 57
  macaroni cheese 29
  pan haggerty 33
  potato & cheese pie 34
  sausage & leek supper 65
  vegetarian moussaka 37
  Welsh rarebit 23
cheesecake, chocolate bar 108
cherries
  Black Forest gateau 111
  boiled fruit Christmas cake 162
  cherry coconut choc traybake 150
  pineapple upside down pudding 119
  tutti frutti ice cream 95
chicken, *as alternative ingredient* 58
  chicken curry 49
  chicken Kiev 50
  coq au vin 53
  coronation chicken sandwiches 20
chocolate, *as alternative ingredient* 99, 115
  Black Forest gateau 111

cherry coconut choc traybake 150
choc mint bars 149
chocolate bar cheesecake 108
chocolate bar fudge 169
chocolate ice cream roll 96
chocolate peppermint creams 169
chocolate pudding 124
chocolate sponge pudding 120
chocolate upside down pudding 119
hedgehog celebration cake 161
krispie cakes 165
milk chocolate fudge 169
school chocolate cracknel 127
tiffin 166
white chocolate fudge 169
Christmas cake, boiled fruit 162
chutney
    chicken curry 49
    coronation chicken sandwiches 20
coconut
    cherry coconut choc traybake 150
    coconut 'grass' 99
    coconut ice 170
    coconut jam sponge pudding 115
    Manchester tart 145
    pineapple & coconut fruit loaf 158
cod with parsley/butter sauce 41
coffee, as alternative ingredient 99
coq au vin 53
corned beef hash 77
coronation chicken sandwiches 20
courgettes, vegetarian moussaka 37
crispy pancakes 58
crumble, fruit 135
currants, fruit slice 146
curry
    chicken 49
    vegetable 49
custard
    baked custards 131
    fruit Pavlova 103
    Manchester tart 145
    pink, green or chocolate custard 127
    strawberry trifle 107

damsons, as alternative ingredient 116
    fruit crumble 135
duck, as alternative ingredient 77

eggs
    baked custards 131
    broccoli & Stilton quiche 57
    buck rarebit 23
    corned beef hash 77

family fish pie 45
finnan haddock 42
leek & cheese quiche 57
quiche Lorraine 57
sausage & pickle pie 66
Eve's pudding 116

family fish pie 45
farmhouse mince 78
finnan haddock 42
fish, as alternative ingredient 58
    cod with parsley sauce 41
    cod with butter sauce 41
    family fish pie 45
    finnan haddock 42
French onion soup with cheese toasts 15
fruit, as alternative ingredient 131
    autumn pudding 104
    fruit crumble 135
    fruit Pavlova 103
    summer pudding 104
fruit, dried, as alternative ingredient 131, 150
    boiled fruit Christmas cake 162
    bread & butter pudding 132
    coronation chicken sandwiches 20
    fruit slice 146
    fruit sponge pudding (spotted dick) 120
    pineapple & coconut fruit loaf 158
    rock cakes 154
    Shrewsbury biscuits 153
    spotted dick 123
    tiffin 166
    tutti frutti ice cream 95
fudge 169

gammon, ham with pease pudding 61
ginger, as alternative ingredient 95, 107, 124, 166
gooseberries, as alternative ingredient 116
    fruit crumble 135
green beans, as alternative ingredient 49

ham, as alternative ingredient 33
    crispy pancakes 58
    ham with pease pudding 61
    split pea & ham soup 19
hedgehog celebration cake 161
honey, as alternative ingredient 99

ice cream
    Arctic roll 96
    chocolate ice cream roll 96
    tutti frutti ice cream 95

jam
    Bakewell tart 142
    coconut jam sponge pudding 115
    jam roly poly 123
    jam sponge pudding 120
    Manchester tart 145
kale, *as alternative ingredient* 30
kidneys
    Lancashire hotpot 73
    steak & kidney pudding 89
krispie cakes 165

lamb, *as alternative ingredient* 30, 77
    Lancashire hotpot 73
    roast lamb with fresh mint sauce 70
    shepherd's pie 74
Lancashire hotpot 73
leeks
    leek & bacon stovies 54
    leek & cheese quiche 57
    leek & potato soup 16
    sausage & leek supper 65
lemons, *as alternative ingredient* 99, 131, 139
    lemon meringue pie 112
    lemon roly poly 123
lentils, farmhouse mince 78
liver & bacon with onion gravy 69
lobby 85

macaroni cheese 29
Manchester tart 145
Mars bar, krispie cakes 165
melba toast 24
mincemeat roly poly 123
moussaka, vegetarian 37
mushrooms, *as alternative ingredient* 58
    beef Stroganoff 86
    coq au vin 53
    creamed mushrooms 12
    Lancashire hotpot 73
    steak Diane 90

nuts, *as alternative ingredient* 95
    Bakewell tart 142
    boiled fruit Christmas cake 162
    coronation chicken sandwiches 20
    veggie burgers 38

onions
    French onion soup with cheese toasts 15
    liver & bacon with onion gravy 69
    mincc & onion pic 81

oranges, *as alternative ingredient* 99, 124
    baked custards 131
Osborne pudding 132
pan haggerty 33
pancakes, crispy 58
parsnips, *as alternative ingredient* 30, 54
pasta, macaroni cheese 29
pearl barley, *as alternative ingredient* 85
pears, *as alternative ingredient* 104, 107, 119
peas, family fish pie 45
peppermint creams 169
pickle, sausage & pickle pie 66
pies, savoury
    family fish pie 45
    mince & onion pie 81
    potato & cheese pie 34
    sausage & pickle pie 66
    shepherd's pie 74
    Teviotdale pie 82
pies, sweet
    butterscotch apple pie 136
    lemon meringue pie 112
pineapple
    pineapple & coconut fruit loaf 158
    pineapple upside down pudding 119
plums, *as alternative ingredient* 104, 116
    fruit crumble 135
potatoes
    bubble & squeak 30
    corned beef hash 77
    family fish pie 45
    Lancashire hotpot 73
    leek & bacon stovies 54
    leek & potato soup 16
    lobby 85
    pan haggerty 33
    potato & cheese pie 34
    sausage & leek supper 65
    scampi & chips 46
    shepherd's pie 74
    split pea & ham soup 19
    vegetarian moussaka 37
potted beef 24
potted shrimps 24
prawns, scampi & chips 46
puddings
    Arctic roll 96
    baked custards 131
    blancmange 99
    bread & butter pudding 132
    butterscotch delight 100
    chocolate pudding 124
    chocolate sponge pudding 120

coconut jam sponge pudding 115
Eve's pudding 116
fruit crumble 135
fruit Pavlova 103
fruit sponge pudding (spotted dick) 120
jam roly poly 123
jam sponge pudding 120
Osborne pudding 132
pineapple upside down pudding 119
rice pudding 128
sago pudding 128
school chocolate cracknel 127
semolina pudding 128
spotted dick 123
strawberry trifle 107
summer pudding 104
syrup sponge pudding 120
tapioca pudding 128

quiche Lorraine 57
Quorn, *as alternative ingredient* 20

raspberries, *as alternative ingredient* 107
rhubarb, *as alternative ingredient* 116
    fruit crumble 135
Rice Krispies, krispie cakes 165
rice pudding 128
rock cakes 154

sago pudding 128
sausages
    sausage & leek supper 65
    sausage & pickle pie 66
    toad-in-the-hole 62
scampi & chips 46
school chocolate cracknel 127
semolina pudding 128
shepherd's pie 74
Shrewsbury biscuits 153
shrimps, potted 24
soups
    French onion soup with cheese toasts 15
    leek & potato soup 16
    split pea & ham soup 19
    vichyssoise 16
spinach, *as alternative ingredient* 49
split peas
    ham with pease pudding 61
    split pea & ham soup 19
spotted dick 120, 123
steak & kidney pudding 89
steak Diane 90
stovies, leek & bacon 54
strawberry trifle 107

suet
    roly poly 123
    steak & kidney pudding 89
    Teviotdale pie 82
summer pudding 104
swede, *as alternative ingredient* 54, 74
    family fish pie 45
    lobby 85
sweet potato, *as alternative ingredient* 45, 54
sweetcorn, *as alternative ingredient* 58
    family fish pie 45
sweets
    butterscotch 170
    chocolate bar fudge 169
    chocolate peppermint creams 169
    coconut ice 170
    milk chocolate fudge 169
    peppermint creams 169
    white chocolate fudge 169
sweetshop celebration cake 161
syrup sponge pudding 120

tapioca pudding 128
tarts
    Bakewell tart 142
    Manchester tart 145
    treacle tart 139
Teviotdale pie 82
tiffin 166
toad-in-the-hole 62
tomatoes, *as alternative ingredient* 74
    vegetarian moussaka 37
Tottenham cake 157
treacle tart 139
trifle 107
tutti frutti ice cream 95

vegetable curry 49
vegetarian moussaka 37
veggie burgers 38
vichyssoise 16
vol au vents, creamed mushrooms 12

Welsh rarebit 23
white chocolate fudge 169

yogurt
    chicken curry 49
    coronation chicken sandwiches 20
Yorkshire pudding, toad-in-the-hole 62

THANKS TO

Market Researcher & Brand Manager	Katy Hackforth
Commissioning/Managing Editor	Emily Davenport
Designers	Steve Scanlan
	Elzani Smit
Copy Editor	Cara Kelsall
Editor	Maggie Ramsay
Photographer	Steve Lee
Food Stylist	Sian Davies
Props Stylist	Olivia Axson
Recipes	Emily Davenport
	Katy Hackforth
	Sian Davies
Recipe Testers	Joanna Leese
	Hannah Nadin
Nutrition Consultant	Sue Baic
Proof Reader	Aune Butt
Indexer	Ruth Ellis
Production Manager	Siobhan Hennessy

DAIRY DIARY
COOK
BOOK

Published by Dairy Diary, a subsidiary of Trek Logistics Ltd

Dairy Diary, PO Box 482, Crewe, CW1 9FG

www.dairydiary.co.uk

First printed May 2024

© Trek Logistics Ltd

ISBN 9781911388517